# THE
# ETERNAL WISDOM

# THE ETERNAL WISDOM

A concise and complete
presentation of the Faith,
illustrated with 180 masterpieces of art.

*Planned by*
**Rev. James Alberione, S.S.P., S.T.D.**

*Compiled by*
**Rev. Eugene Fornasari, S.S.P.**
*Translated and adapted for the United States*
*by the*
**Daughters of St. Paul**

ST. PAUL EDITIONS

NIHIL OBSTAT:
Rev. Richard V. Lawlor, S.J.
*Censor*

IMPRIMATUR:
✠Humberto Cardinal Medeiros
*Archbishop of Boston*

ISBN 0-8198-2310-4 cloth
0-8198-2311-2 paper



---

Printed in the U.S.A. by the Daughters of St. Paul
50 St. Paul's Ave., Boston, MA 02130

The Daughters of St. Paul are an international congregation of religious women serving the Church with the communications media.

## FOREWORD

We come from the hands of God, we are traveling toward heaven, and at the end of our lives we shall receive that which we have merited on earth. We need faith to live by. To whom shall we go if not to the only Master and Teacher who has words of eternal wisdom? Jesus Christ said: "I am the Way, the Truth, and the Life."

The religion of Jesus Christ has always been the driving force behind the deeds of great men and women.

The purpose of the present book, *The Eternal Wisdom*, is to make the teachings of our divine Savior and His Church better known, followed, and loved.

# CONTENTS

PART I

# THE PRINCIPAL TRUTHS OF FAITH

***Who made us?***
**God made us.**

"God created man to his own image; to the image of God he created him. Male and female he created them. And he blessed them, saying, 'Increase and multiply, and fill the earth and subdue it'" (Gn. 1:27-28).

In solemn words, Sacred Scripture tells us that after creating this beautiful earth with its vast oceans, snow-capped peaks, and level plains, the Almighty God created man and gave him dominion over all created things.

The first man and woman, Adam and Eve, were the first parents of the whole human race. Their souls were created directly by God, as is every human soul.

"Man is a noble being created to the image and likeness of God, not as regards his body, but in that he excels the brute animals because of the gift of a rational soul," explains St. Augustine. And St. Thomas Aquinas says further, "Man excels all animals by his reason and intelligence; thus, it is because of his intelligence and reason, which are spiritual, that man is said to have been created according to the image of God."

**God created me:** how sublime is this thought. I did not exist, and God, who is so great and good, thought of me and created me. My life, therefore, is valuable and important, and it is for me to esteem it so, and to use it worthily.

**"Happy the man who delights in the law of the Lord and meditates on his law day and night."**
cf. Psalm 1:2

*St. Paul the Apostle in Prayer* Bartolini

*The Father Creating* Schnorr

***Who is God?***

**God is the Supreme Being, infinitely perfect, who made all things and keeps them in existence.**

***What do we mean when we say that God is infinitely perfect?***

**When we say that God is infinitely perfect we mean that He has all perfections without limit.**

All created things, by their very existence, show forth the glory of God, their Creator. God, in His exceeding goodness, wished certain things to come into existence which would enjoy His benefits and share in His goodness. He brought all things out of nothing into being and He preserves them; otherwise they would again sink into nothing.

God is above all His creatures, the self-existing and infinitely perfect Spirit. He has in Himself, in an eminent degree, the perfections of all things that ever existed or will or can exist. All the goodness, beauty, wisdom and power we admire in creatures are but the merest shadow of the goodness, beauty, wisdom, and power of God.

To understand fully who God is, we would need an infinite intelligence—we would have to be God Himself.

**"It is indeed a great thing for God to have given us our very existence; but it will be a far greater thing for us to have found our rest in Him."**

St. Augustine

*The Lord God* Schnorr

***What do we mean when we say that God is the Creator of heaven and earth?***

**When we say that God is the Creator of heaven and earth we mean that He made all things from nothing by His almighty power.**

**"In the beginning God created heaven and earth"** (Gn. 1:1). Sacred Scripture, inspired by the Holy Spirit, opens with the vision of God, the Creator.

To create means to **make from nothing.** Only God can create, because creation requires infinite power, which God alone possesses. By a single act of His will, He brought every living being into life. "He commanded and they were created" (Ps. 148:4).

Men cannot create; they can only construct. A sculptor needs marble for his statue; a painter needs canvas; a carpenter, wood. God needed nothing to create all things. Men are capable of many things, but their powers are, nevertheless, limited. Only God is omnipotent.

"The very order, disposition, beauty, change, and motion of the world and of all visible things proclaim that it could only have been made by God, the ineffably and invisibly great and the ineffably and invisibly beautiful" (St. Augustine).

**"Nature reveals its Author, the work suggests the Artist, and the world manifests its Designer."**

St. Irenaeus

*St. Mary of Egypt* Tintorello-Anderson

***What do we mean when we say that God is all-present?***

**When we say that God is all-present we mean that He is everywhere.**

Tintorello's meaningful painting of St. Mary of Egypt in the solitude of the Jordan floods our souls with inexpressible emotion.

Before her conversion, Mary was a great sinner. One day she joined a group of pilgrims going to Jerusalem to venerate the holy cross, but upon reaching the Holy City she could not enter the temple; a mysterious force repelled her. When she finally understood that her unworthiness was the sole cause of her rejection, she burst into tears, promising the Blessed Virgin that she would do penance. From that day on she changed her life. Retiring into solitude, she spent almost fifty years performing the most austere types of penance. The thought of the divine Presence animated and comforted her.

God is everywhere by His **power,** inasmuch as all things are under His dominion; by His **presence,** inasmuch as nothing is hidden from Him; by His **essence** inasmuch as He is in all things as the cause of their being. "Do I not fill heaven and earth?" says the Lord (Jer. 23:24).

"The eyes of the Lord in every place behold the good and the evil" (Prv. 15:3). The thought of God's presence helps us overcome temptation and avoid sin; it dispels anger, greediness, boredom, and distractions.

One who remembers that God, our loving Father, is ever near, can never be lonely or broken by sorrow.

The continual remembrance of God's presence makes a soul quickly attain to the highest perfection.

**"I am the Almighty God; walk before me and be perfect."** Gn. 17:1

*God in the Burning Bush* Schnorr

***If God is everywhere, why do we not see Him?***

**Although God is everywhere, we do not see Him because He is a spirit and cannot be seen with our eyes.**

Sacred Scripture narrates that Moses, the great leader of God's people, one day led his flock to pasture at the foot of Mount Horeb. Suddenly, raising his eyes to the summit, he saw great flames leaping from a bush which burned without being destroyed. Since his curiosity was aroused, he was about to draw closer, to see the wonder, when he heard the Lord's voice calling him.

God was present in those flames, but invisible to Moses' eyes. In order to have an idea of God, we must represent Him in a human manner: with body, face and arms, but He does not really have a body.

Within us is a soul which makes us see, feel, walk and think. When anyone dies he does not see, feel or walk any longer, because the soul has left his body. We never see the soul, because it is a spirit, just as we never see our guardian angels, who are also pure spirits.

Thus God is present everywhere; He penetrates us with His divine essence; He guides and governs us by His ineffable Providence.

**"In him we live and move and have our being; for we also are his offspring."**
Acts 17:28

*The Eternal Father* Fra Bartolomeo-Alinari

***What do we mean when we say that God is eternal?***

**When we say that God is eternal we mean that He always was and always will be, and that He always remains the same.**

The world is many, many centuries old. Before it came to be, no one existed except God—God who was never born, who always was.

Men grow old and die, as have all others before them; one day even the world and the rest of the universe will come to an end—but God will never die, He will never have an end. He will always live.

**" 'I am Alpha and Omega,' says the Lord, 'the first and the last' "** (Rv. 22:13). In the picture, God is represented as a venerable old man. In order to indicate His agelessness, He is seated on the waves of time holding in His hand the book of life, in which are written the first and last letters of the Greek alphabet, Alpha and Omega. God is the beginning and end of everything.

The sun rises and sets; the pendulum ticks off the fleeting hours; years and seasons pass without pausing. Only God is unchanging. For Him, there is neither past nor future; He is always present in His eternity.

We, God's children, are not eternal; we are **immortal.** Our soul, being spiritual, does not die with our body but lives forever; and even the body will rise one day—to be united with the soul in its eternal life.

**"O Lord! my heart is sick,**
**Sick of this everlasting change;**
**And life runs tediously quick**
**Through its unresting race and varied range:**
**Change finds no likeness to itself in Thee,**
**And wakes no echo in Thy mute eternity."**

Father Faber

*Jonah* Dorè-Garzanti

***What do we mean when we say that God is all-knowing?***

**When we say that God is all-knowing we mean that He knows all things, past, present and future, even our most secret thoughts, words and actions.**

Jonah, the prophet, lived among God's chosen people. One day the Lord called him, commanding him to go to the great city of Nineveh, where there were many sinners to be converted.

Not wanting to obey the Lord's command, Jonah boarded a ship sailing in the opposite direction, whereupon the Lord became angry with him, and a great storm rose at sea threatening to sink the vessel.

Repenting of his fault, the prophet begged the sailors to throw him overboard so that they themselves might be saved. They did so, and God sent a whale to swallow him. Then from the bottom of his heart Jonah begged the Lord to free him, and God heard his prayer. After three days the whale returned him safe and sound to the shore near Nineveh. There the prophet fulfilled the mission which had been entrusted to him by God.

God sees all and knows all—in the brightness of daylight and the darkness of night. He knows even the most hidden things—our most intimate thoughts, what we feel in the depths of our hearts.

He knows everything past and future, for God is omniscient.

When all alone and tempted to commit sin, let us remember that the Lord is watching us, that He sees into the most secret depths of our souls and that one day He will judge us. How can we escape the Lord's gaze?

**"If I ascend into heaven, you are there; if I lie down with the dead, you are there."** Ps. 139:8

*The Multiplication of Loaves* Murillo-Anderson

***What do we mean when we say that God is almighty?***

**When we say that God is almighty we mean that He can do all things.**

We cannot always do as we wish. An old proverb says that the grass of wishes does not even grow in the gardens of kings.

But God, the Creator and Lord of all things, can do everything He desires at each moment.

All the forces of nature, of life and death, of the sky, the earth and even of hell are ready at His command.

A miracle is a sign of God's omnipotence, because it surpasses the forces of nature. How many miracles Jesus performed when He was on earth! One such miracle was the multiplication of the loaves:

More than five thousand people had been following Jesus in the desert for three days. They were hungry, but there was nothing to eat. Only one little boy had brought with him five loaves and two fishes.

Jesus blessed the loaves and the fishes—and they increased and were multiplied by the thousands, so that after all the people had eaten of them and were satisfied there was still enough bread left over to fill seven baskets!

Wonders of God's power! It is He who provides for the needs of our life.

With great confidence let us often repeat this beautiful prayer:
**"By myself I can do nothing, but with God I can do everything!"**

*Joseph Sold* Schnorr

***For what do we pray when we say, "but deliver us from evil"?***

**When we say "but deliver us from evil," we pray that God will always protect us from harm, and especially from harm to our souls.**

God is infinite goodness. Good and bad cannot remain together. Desiring and doing evil is not perfection, but rather defect, and in God, who is the all-perfect being, there are no imperfections.

Sin is real evil. Therefore, God can neither commit sin nor will it, because it is an offense against Him, and He cannot offend Himself. However, He permits it in creatures of free will. But, just as doctors have learned how to extract precious medicines from the most fatal poisons, so can God derive good even from evil.

As a boy, Joseph the Hebrew was so good that his father, Jacob, favored him; for this reason, his brothers burned with envy and hatred. One day when they were tending their sheep far from home, they saw Joseph coming, and seizing him, they imprisoned him in a dark pit. When some Arab merchants came by, they sold their brother to them for a few pieces of silver.

But God knew how to derive great good from the afflictions of the virtuous boy. Joseph was led into Egypt; he was chosen governor of that country by the Pharoah, and in a time of great trial he helped all the people, including his father and even his brothers.

Because we are weak, we often follow our own bad inclinations. Let us beg the Lord for the grace to avoid evil and to want to do only good.

**"Sin is a fearful evil, but not incurable; fearful for him who clings to it, but easy to cure for him who by repentance puts it from him."**

St. Cyril

*Hagar in the Desert* Dorè-Garzanti

***What is God's loving care for us called?***
**God's loving care for us is called divine Providence.**

A woman named Hagar was lost and wandering about the desert with her child. There was no water, and her son was dying of thirst. Finally the poor mother laid the boy on the ground and departed in tears, so as not to see him die. But the child's cries reached the heavens, and God sent His angel to show Hagar a miraculous spring which came up from the sand to quench both her thirst and the little boy's.

How good God is! He never abandons His creatures, but provides food for the birds and bread for the poor. He gives us strength and health, sunlight and rain, flowers in the spring, warmth in summer, and fruit in autumn; in the winter time He makes seeds germinate beneath the snow. Just as a mother carries her baby, so does Providence bear us in its arms.

God is **infinite wisdom;** He guides us to the end for which He has destined us. As **infinite goodness,** He has prepared paradise for us that we may be happy forever. He is **infinite power,** and He offers us all the means to attain heaven. As **infinite justice,** He will reward the good and punish the bad.

Even suffering is an instrument which God uses either to guide souls or to recall them to the way of salvation. St. Thérèse of the Child Jesus exclaimed, "I thank You, Lord, for having made me pass through the crucible of so much suffering!"

**"Bodily suffering, borne with fortitude, purifies the souls that are good."**

St. Augustine

*St. Paul in the Imperial Palace* De Martini-Anderson

***What must we do to gain the happiness of heaven?***

**To gain the happiness of heaven we must know, love and serve God in this world.**

A child, who develops in life as a tender bud in the sun's rays, storms his parents with his "why?" He wants to know. The soul desires truth, especially the first and supreme Truth which is God. However, many do not know the Lord! A large part of humanity is still immersed in the dark night of paganism and idolatry. Even many Christians, through a deplorable life, have lost the light of faith and the uprightness of mind which make one know God. Poor unfortunates! Without the desire to know God, one will never attain to the conquest of truth.

Observe the thought-provoking scene shown in the illustration. Even in chains, Christ's tireless Apostle, Paul, preached the doctrine of Christ to both the humble and powerful, in huts and palaces alike. He even dared to cross the threshold of Nero's palace, where the emperor's praetors, servants and slaves listened intently to the Apostle's inflamed words, and were enraptured by the sublimity of the Christian religion—which alone can satisfy the deepest needs of the human spirit.

We are created to know God, to possess eternal life, to be submerged in the beatific vision of the Most High.

**"Now this is everlasting life," said Jesus, "that they may know you, the only true God and him whom you have sent, Jesus Christ."** Jn. 17:3

*The Martyrdom of St. Agnes* Guercino-Anderson

***What are we to do to gain the happiness of heaven?***

**To gain the happiness of heaven, we must know, love, and serve God in this world.**

Man's heart longs to love the known good, and since God is the supreme Good which the human mind can know, the heart should burn with love for the Creator.

The human heart palpitates with superhuman desires. No creature can satisfy it; God alone can completely fulfill our yearning for love.

"O God, You have created us for Yourself, and our heart is restless until it rests in You!" sighed St. Augustine.

Saints are wise persons who make God's love the reason for their lives, their labors, their martyrdom. Observe the Roman martyr, St. Agnes, in the illustration. Already a wonderful girl at the age of thirteen, she was sought in marriage by the Roman Prefect's son, Procopius. Agnes refused. Her heart could not belong to a man. "Oh, Procopius, I love Christ! I have consecrated myself to Him; I shall be His forever!"

The refusal of Agnes infuriated the young man whose love changed to hate, and he denounced her to his father as a Christian. Agnes, dragged to an infamous place, was defended by an angel; condemned to burn, she miraculously escaped the flames; at last, the axe descended to cut off her virginal head. The angelic girl fell exclaiming, "I already possess what I desired; now I shall be united in heaven to Him whom I loved on earth with all my strength."

To love God is a duty—a necessity for the soul, which is an object of infinite predilection on God's part.

**"You shall love the Lord your God," said the Lord, "with your whole heart, and with your whole soul, and with your whole mind. This is the greatest and the first commandment."** Mt. 22:37

*The Works and Grace of Christian Life* Seitz-Anderson

***Why did God make us?***

**God made us to show forth His goodness and to share with us His everlasting happiness in heaven.**

Just as a faithful servant waits on his master, trying sincerely to please him, so does a Christian serve God by applying himself serenely to do His most holy will, which is expressed by the commandments, divine inspirations, circumstances, and the duties of one's state in life.

**"Not every one who says to me, 'Lord, Lord,' shall enter the kingdom of heaven; but he who does the will of my Father in heaven"** (Mt. 7:21).

Blessed are they who serve God faithfully! For them He reserves an inexpressibly great reward.

Note how the picture illustrates God's service being performed by holy souls. In the center is St. Isidore, a humble farmer who, consoled by the angels, sanctifies his generous work. At the left St. Paul gives an incomparable example of penitential life in the solitude of the desert, while St. Veronica Giuliani, seraph of the Eucharist, edifies her religious sisters in the cloister. At the right, St. Charles Borromeo, Archbishop of Milan, serves God through the sick poor, while Peter the Hermit spurs the crowds on to the Crusades with his inflamed sermons and the cry, "God wants it!"

Let us, too, serve God by faithfully fulfilling our duties. It will be this faithful service that will one day win us the eternal reward:

**"Well done, good and faithful servant! Enter into the joy of your Master!"**
Mt. 25:23

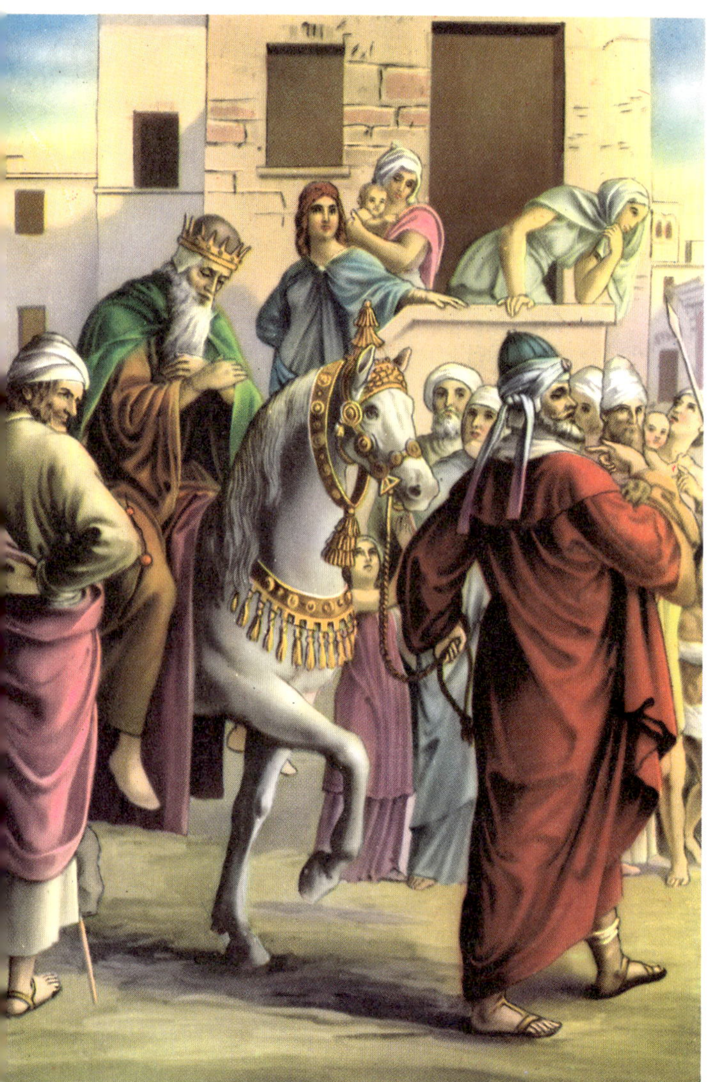

*The Triumph of Mordecai* Schnorr

***What are the rewards or punishments appointed for men after the particular judgment?***

**The rewards or punishments appointed for men after the particular judgment are heaven, purgatory, or hell.**

Justice demands that good be rewarded and evil be punished. Now, God is not only just but He is infinite Justice, and for this reason He rewards the good with paradise and punishes the wicked with hell.

Sacred Scripture narrates that a pious Israelite named Mordecai had saved the life of the powerful King, Ahasuerus, by revealing to him a wicked conspiracy plotted against him. Long after this, Haman, the King's powerful minister, became indignant against Mordecai because he did not bow to honor him when passing by; therefore he obtained from the King an edict which condemned all the people of Judea to be massacred.

At that very time, the King remembered that Mordecai had saved his life, and desired to reward him. Haman himself had to lead his rival through the city, crowned and dressed in kingly robes and riding a magnificent steed. Furthermore, King Ahasuerus, learning of Haman's wicked plan, condemned him to the same punishment he had prepared for Mordecai.

The Lord is just, and **He will render** to everyone the reward or punishment deserved as the Prophet sings:

**"You are just, O Lord, and your judgment is right."** Ps. 119:137

*The Death of St. Joseph* Franceschini-Alinari

***Who are rewarded in heaven?***

**Those are rewarded in heaven who have died in the state of grace and have been purified in purgatory, if necessary, from all venial sin and all debt of temporal punishment.**

Heaven is a reward. God gives paradise to those who love and serve Him faithfully and die in His grace, that is, in His friendship, being without serious sin.

The illustration reproduces St. Joseph's happy death. The holy Gospel says that he was a just man, gifted with every virtue. How much sweetness must have flooded his soul when he felt so close to the eternal reward and his mortal life was ending in the purest love, filled with the comfort of Jesus and Mary!

There have been many people who have loved Jesus very much. They were generous, pure and diligent in their duties, and have already merited the reward of paradise.

How happy they must be!

Let us have courage and do as they did. Grace and good will are needed.

Remember the words that the heroic mother of the Maccabees addressed to her son, tortured for his faith:

**"I beseech you, my son, look upon heaven!"** 2 Mc. 7:28

*Paradise* De Matteis-Alinari

***What do the blessed enjoy in heaven?***

**They see God face to face and share forever in His glory and happiness.**

There is no place on this earth where one never weeps, where there is no pain or sorrow, where one never dies, but is happy forever. There are many miseries on earth; that is why it is called a valley of tears.

However, God created us to be happy forever; not here, but in paradise, His home. There the Virgin Mary, all the angels, and all the saints rejoice in singing the Lord's praises. They see God, and love Him with a love which is far beyond our power to imagine. The happiness they have will never end. It will be eternal!

**"Earth has no sorrow that heaven cannot heal."** Thomas More

**"O paradise! O paradise!**
**Who does not crave for rest?**
**Who would not seek the happy land**
**Where they that love are blest?**
**Where loyal hearts and true,**
**Stand ever in the light,**
**All rapture through and through**
**In God's most holy sight!"** Father Faber

***Who are punished in purgatory?***

**Those are punished for a time in purgatory who die in the state of grace but are guilty of venial sin, or have not fully made satisfaction for the temporal punishment due to their sins.**

*Purgatory* Guercino-Alinari

Some sins are more serious than others. Grievous sins merit hell, whereas less serious sins, as also the unremitted temporal punishment due to sin, deserve purgatory.

Purgatory is a place of painful suffering, where souls who have departed from this life with some debt of punishment for sins committed, or with some venial sin still unpardoned, purify themselves to become worthy to ascend to heaven.

In purgatory there are the "pain of fire" and many other punishments, but they do not last eternally, and those blessed souls are resigned, because they are certain of some day seeing God again and of being happy with Him.

We can shorten the sufferings of the souls in purgatory by offering them our help. From the earliest times, attested the holy Pontiff, Gregory the Great, it was a pious custom in the Church to offer the holy Sacrifice of the Mass for the deceased. God willingly accepts our prayers, frees those holy souls, and opens the gates of heaven to them.

Before her death, St. Monica said to her son, St. Augustine, "This only I ask of you: that you should remember me at the altar of the Lord wherever you may be."

**"It is therefore a holy and wholesome thought to pray for the dead, that they may be loosed from sins."** Mc. 12:46

*Lazarus* Dorè-Treves

***Who are punished in hell?***

**Those are punished in hell who die in mortal sin.**

Jesus tells us that there was a wealthy man who wore royal clothes and had splendid banquets with his friends every day. And there was a beggar named Lazarus, covered with wounds, who lay at the rich man's door, desirous of satisfying his hunger with the crumbs that fell from the table, but no one gave them to him. Only the dogs came to lick his sores.

Lazarus died and was carried to Abraham's bosom by the angels. The rich man died, too, and was buried in hell. Lifting his eyes on high in the midst of torments, he saw the happiness of Lazarus, and cried: "Father Abraham, have pity on me. Send Lazarus to dip the tip of his finger in water so as to refresh my tongue, for I suffer in these flames!" But Abraham answered, "Son, remember that while you received many goods in life you closed your heart to your brothers' needs. Lazarus, instead, had only ills, and bore them with great patience. There is also such a great gulf between you and us, that it is possible neither for us to come there, nor for you to come to us" (cf. Lk. 16:26).

There is a **great gulf** between **good** and **evil,** as there is between God and the sinner. Goodness deserves a reward; evil deserves punishment.

**"Enter by the narrow gate," Jesus warns us, "for wide is the gate, and broad is the way that leads to destruction, and many there are who enter that way."**

Mt. 7:13

***What do the damned suffer in hell?***

**In hell the damned are deprived of the vision of God and suffer dreadful torments, especially that of fire, for all eternity.**

The illustration depicts with dramatic power the noiseless and desperate precipitation of the damned into the pits of hell, dazzled by the terrible sentence of the divine Judge: **"Depart from me, accursed ones, into the everlasting fire"** (Mt. 25:41).

After death, the soul is attracted to God as iron is drawn to a magnet. But God rejects it. The soul did not want to serve Him in life, so it will be deprived of Him eternally.

Hell is the "place of torments." The essential torment is the awareness of being separated forever from God. The damned also suffer pains of sense.

*Hell* Rubens-Alinari

We do not know the exact nature of the pain of fire in hell or purgatory. Whatever it is, the punishment will fit the crime.

But the most tormenting pain will be the absence of God, the sum total good desired by the soul with desperate nostalgia. This pain is for the damned one an **eternal death** which every instant, for infinite centuries, deprives him of the true life of the soul, God.

**"Hell is where no one has anything in common with anybody else except the fact that they all hate one another and cannot get away from one another and from themselves."** Thomas Merton

*The Angels' Apparition to Abraham* Tiepolo-Fiorentini

***Is there only one God?***

**Yes, there is only one God.**

***How many Persons are there in God?***

**In God there are three divine Persons—the Father, the Son, and the Holy Spirit.**

Sacred Scripture narrates that one day Abraham was visited by three angels in human form. Abraham prostrated himself reverently before the unexpected apparition and **adored God** saying, **"Lord, if I have found favor in your sight, pass not away from your servant"** (Gn. 18:3). And the three angels stood still and promised Abraham that his wife Sarah would soon give birth to Isaac, the son of the promise.

Abraham saw three persons and he adored only one God. Why? The mystery of the most Holy Trinity, some suggest, was foreshadowed in the apparition.

We know that there is only one God. He revealed this Himself, **"I am the one true God and there is no God beside me"** (Is. 46:9).

But by an unspeakable mystery, in God, who is **one** in **nature,** there are **three** perfectly equal and distinct **Persons.**

The Gospel continually speaks of the **Son** of God made man, of His heavenly **Father** and of the **Holy Spirit.** Before ascending to heaven, Jesus expressly ordered the Apostles to "make disciples of all nations, baptizing them in the **name of the Father, and of the Son, and of the Holy Spirit"** (Mt. 28:19).

**Let us join the seraphs in heaven who endlessly sing to the one and triune God, "Holy, holy, holy is the Lord God of hosts."** Is. 6:3

***Is the Father God?***

**The Father is God and the first Person of the Blessed Trinity.**

Note the majestic power with which Dorè enlivens the figure of God the Father, the Source of light and life.

The Father is the first Person of the most Holy Trinity because He proceeds from no other Person.

The Father, like the Son and the Holy Spirit, is eternal.

Although all His perfections and actions are common to the other divine Persons, power and creation are attributed to Him.

By His almighty power, the heavenly Father has created the sky, the earth, light, plants, animals and man—everything that exists.

He also creates each soul and governs all His creatures, sustaining them in life and providing them with means of support.

*The Father* Dorè-Garzanti

Father! The name contains a poem of love. All the tenderness of all fathers of the earth for their children can give us only a faint idea of God's love for us.

Out of love, He gave us life; He wants us to share His eternal happiness in heaven, and in order to save us after man's first sin, He did not hesitate to send His beloved Son to earth.

In return, we must love the heavenly Father with all our hearts.

**"There is a twofold reason why God should be loved for His own sake: because nothing else can be more justly or more profitably loved."**

St. Bernard

*Jesus Christ* Carracci-Alinari

***Is the Son God?***

**The Son is God and the second Person of the Blessed Trinity.**

Look at Jesus in the composed and tranquil beauty of His humanity as depicted by Carracci's art. Jesus, Son of the heavenly Father, is the second Person of the Blessed Trinity, who became man to save us.

The Son of God is also called the **Word,** and **Eternal Wisdom,** because He proceeds from the Father by way of knowledge. From all eternity, the Father knows Himself; His act of knowing Himself produces an Idea, a Word; and this Idea, this Word that the Father generates, is infinite, eternal, living, a Person—the second Person of the Blessed Trinity, equal in all things to the Father. To Him are attributed the works of wisdom, the world's order and its preservation.

**"He,"** says St. Paul, **"is the image of the invisible God, and the firstborn of every creature; all things have been created through him and unto him."** Col. 1:15-17

The Gospel of St. John opens with this solemn prelude, **"In the beginning was the Word, and the Word was with God, and the Word was God. And the Word was made flesh, and dwelt among us."** Jn. 1:1, 14

The Father Himself testified, in the Transfiguration on the mount, that Jesus Christ is the Incarnate Word, begotten by the Father: **"This is my beloved Son; hear Him."** Mk. 9:5

**"When the grasp upon Christ's divinity is sure and unfaltering, there is no danger that an intimate affection for His humanity will lead souls astray."**

R. H. Benson

***Is the Holy Spirit God?***

**The Holy Spirit is God and the third Person of the Blessed Trinity.**

*The Special Annunciation* Giaquinto-Anderson

The luminous dove, hovering between heaven and earth among a choir of angels, represents the Holy Spirit, the third Person of the most Holy Trinity, who hovered above the head of Jesus the day He was baptized.

The Holy Spirit is the personal and subsistent Love of the Father and Son, proceeding from the Father and the Son as from one principle of love.

The Father and the Son combine in an act of love, and this reciprocal love of Father and Son is subsistent **Love,** that is, the third Person of the Blessed Trinity.

Like the Father and Son, the Holy Spirit is God; equally eternal, uncreated, and omnipotent. The works of love and the sanctification of souls are attributed to the Holy Spirit.

"The Holy Spirit is a Power most mighty, a Being divine and unsearchable; for He is living and intelligent, a sanctifying principle of all things made by God through Christ.... There is one God the Father...and one Lord, Jesus Christ...and one Holy Spirit, who through the prophets preached of Christ, and when Christ was come, descended, and manifested Him" (St. Cyril of Jerusalem).

In the sacraments, especially Confirmation, the Holy Spirit pours His graces and gifts into souls in abundance. This divine grace transforms the soul into a living tabernacle, and the body into a holy temple of the Lord, which must never be profaned by sin.

**"Come, O Holy Spirit, fill the hearts of your faithful and enkindle in them the fire of your love."**

*St. Augustine and the Angel* Sansovino-Brogi

***Can we fully understand how the three divine Persons, though really distinct from one another, are one and the same God?***

**We cannot fully understand how the three divine Persons, though really distinct from one another are one and the same God, because this is a supernatural mystery.**

One day St. Augustine, the great bishop and Doctor of the Church, was walking along the seashore, deeply absorbed in thought. His marvelously keen intellect was trying futilely to analyze the mystery of the Blessed Trinity: the Father is God, the Son is God, the Holy Spirit is God, but all three divine Persons are only one God.

His mind was wandering through the obscurity of the mystery when suddenly there appeared before him a charming little boy who was intently digging in the sand.

"What are you doing, little one?" asked the saint.

"I want to put all the water of the ocean into this little hole."

"It is impossible!" St. Augustine exclaimed. "How can this little hole contain the immensity of the ocean?"

"And how can your feeble mind comprehend God's highest mysteries?" was the reply.

The child disappeared. It had been an angel, and Augustine understood the lesson.

The mystery of the Blessed Trinity is the most sublime mystery of our religion. It surpasses our mind's capacity.

**"The Father is my trust, the Son is my refuge, the Holy Spirit is my protection. O Holy Trinity, glory to You."** Byzantine Horologion

***Did God abandon man after Adam fell into sin?***

**God did not abandon man after Adam fell into sin, but promised to send into the world a Savior to free man from his sins and to reopen to him the gates of heaven.**

*The Blessed Trinity* Murillo-Anderson

Creation is a work of love. From all eternity the three divine Persons lived in intense happiness; but they wanted others to share their blessedness. Thus man was created, endowed with wonderful gifts, placed in a paradise of delight, and raised to the dignity of God's son and king of all creation.

But the story of man is a sorrowful story. At his first trial, he allowed himself to be seduced by the devil; he disobeyed the Creator; he became unworthy of God's grace and friendship and was expelled from paradise.

Original sin, like every mortal sin, being an offense against an infinite God, had infinite malice and provoked swift punishment from divine Justice. Could man, a poor, guilty creature, ever have made reparation? Never!

It was God's infinite love, which had already created man, that was to redeem man. The second Person of the Blessed Trinity, the Son of God, came down to earth. He took on a human nature. He assumed a body and a soul exactly like man's, and He sacrificed Himself for sinful humanity, as a victim of expiation, offering a worthy satisfaction to His eternal Father for every sin.

**"But when the goodness and kindness of God our Savior appeared,"** says St. Paul, **"he saved us through the bath of regeneration and renewal by the Holy Spirit whom he has abundantly poured out upon us through Jesus Christ our Savior."**

Ti. 3:4-5

*St. Peter Cures a Lame Man* Piola-Alinari

***Who is the Savior of all men?***

**The Savior of all men is Jesus Christ.**

When the Archangel Gabriel hastened to the little house in Nazareth and announced to the Blessed Virgin that she was to become the Mother of the Son of God, he stated the name that she would give Him: **"You shall call his name Jesus"** (Lk. 1:31).

The Blessed Virgin was prompt in fulfilling the divine command after the birth of the Savior. She had Him circumcised eight days later and gave Him the name of Jesus.

**Jesus** means Savior; it clearly expresses the mission of the Word Incarnate among men. Jesus came to save what was lost.

Jesus is the **Christ.** Christ is a Greek word which means: the Messiah, the One sent by God, the Lord's anointed One. The name of Jesus Christ is the holiest name, the most glorious, and the sweetest that has ever been invoked on earth. It is balm to the heart and sweetness to our lips in time of sorrow or in the decisive hours of our life.

The miracle illustrated was worked by St. Peter in the name of Jesus. Peter and John were going up to the temple when they met a poor, unfortunate man, crippled from birth, who was begging for alms. Looking upon him with an ardent gaze, Peter said, "Silver and gold I have none; but what I have, that I give you. **In the name of Jesus Christ of Nazareth, arise and walk"** (Acts 3:6). Instantly the beggar sprang to his feet, perfectly cured, and followed the Apostles into the temple—praising God.

Superhuman power of the name of Jesus!

**"There is no other name under heaven,"** affirms St. Peter, **"by which we must be saved."**

Acts 4:12

***What is the chief teaching of the Catholic Church about Jesus Christ?***

**The chief teaching of the Catholic Church about Jesus Christ is that He is God made man.**

*The Baptism of Jesus* Giaquinto-Anderson

The holy Gospel narrates that when Jesus reached the age of thirty, the hour struck for His public life. He bid farewell to the Virgin, His Mother, left Nazareth, and went to the shores of the Jordan where John the Baptist was administering baptism to penitents. Jesus, too, wanted to be baptized. Hardly had He gone into the water, when the heavens above Him opened, the Holy Spirit hovered over His head in the form of a dove, and there came a voice from heaven saying, **"You are my beloved Son"** (Mk. 1:11).

This is the solemn proclamation of the divinity and the mission of Jesus. He is the eternal Word of the Father, the second Person of the Blessed Trinity, who for love of man, the victim of sin, descended into our midst and assumed a body and a soul like ours.

He is the God-Man who represents humanity to the Father, after having redeemed it from the slavery of sin.

In the words of St. Alphonsus, let us thank Jesus for having deigned to assume our very nature and for having become our brother:

**"Great King, from heaven's high throne descending low,**
**In Bethlehem's stable born in cold and woe,**
**You shiver in a manger, Babe Divine,**
**Much have You borne for sins: how much for mine!"**

St. Alphonsus Liguori

*The Magi* Conga-Anderson

***How many natures has Jesus Christ?***

**Jesus Christ has two natures: the nature of God and the nature of man.**

When Jesus was born in Bethlehem, there appeared in the heavens a wondrous star which was seen even in distant countries of the Orient.

There were three great wise men (tradition says they were kings), who understood that the star announced the birth of the Savior whom the world awaited. Desiring to see Him, they left their countries, and, preceded by the star, reached Bethlehem after a long journey. The star stood still exactly over the little house where Jesus, Mary and Joseph were staying.

Entering with great joy, the Magi knelt at the feet of the Infant to adore Him. Then, having opened their treasures, they offered gifts: gold, frankincense, and myrrh. The Fathers of the Church say that gold symbolizes the divine nature of Jesus; myrrh, His human nature; and incense, the homage of prayer to Jesus, God and man.

Jesus is true God because He is the second Person of the Blessed Trinity. Jesus Christ is also true man because He assumed a body and soul like ours. He is, however, but one Person: and this Person is both God and man:

**"Jesus is God! The glorious bands**
**Of golden angels sing**
**Songs of adoring praise to Him**
**Their Maker and their King.**
**He was true God in Bethlehem's crib,**
**On Calvary's cross true God,**
**He who in heaven eternal reigned,**
**In time on earth abode."**

Fr. Faber

*Adam and Eve Driven from Paradise* Schnorr

***What is meant by the redemption?***

**By the redemption is meant that Jesus Christ, as the Redeemer of the whole human race, offered His sufferings and death to God as a fitting sacrifice in satisfaction for our sins, and regained for us the right to be children of God and heirs of heaven.**

God created Adam and Eve and endowed them with wonderful gifts, for He wanted them to be immensely happy, inclined to good, highly intelligent, and free from illness and death. In addition, He gave them the greatest gift of all: grace which made them sons of God and heirs of paradise.

To test their fidelity, God forbade them to eat fruit from the tree of good and evil. But when the devil took the form of a serpent and tempted Eve to pick and eat of that fruit, she listened to him, ate of the fruit, and gave some to Adam; thus, they committed the first sin.

Immediately God punished them. They lost grace and all the other gifts for themselves and for their children. They were expelled from the earthly paradise, and the Lord also closed to them the gates of heaven.

How, then, could men again acquire grace, become God's sons once more, and save themselves?

In order to save us, the heavenly Father sent His divine Son, who redeemed us from sin and reopened the gates of paradise.

The great St. Augustine says that God became man so that we might become like God, or rather, His children.

**"For no one is redeemed except through unmerited mercy, and no one is condemned except through merited judgment."** St. Augustine

*The Crucifixion* — Joseph Janssens-Riv. Die Christiche Kunst

***What do we learn from the sufferings and death of Christ?***

**From the sufferings and death of Christ we learn God's love for man and the evil of sin, for which God, who is all-just, demands such great satisfaction.**

In the illustration, Jesus is hanging from the cross—pierced and bleeding. Behold what He did to save us! He willed to expiate our sins and offer His eternal Father a worthy reparation for the offense committed against Him.

Jesus was God and man. As man, He willed to suffer and die on the cross in order to acquire merit just as if He were one of us, since, as God, He could neither suffer nor die. And as God, He gave to His merits an infinite value. He satisfied the Father's justice and thus reopened heaven to us.

Furthermore, He taught us by His word and example, confirmed by miracles, to live not according to our bad inclinations and the false maxims of the world, but according to God. He taught us the divine truths which we must believe and practice in order to please Him and merit heaven after this life.

**"Seek first the kingdom of God and his justice, and all these things shall be given you besides."** Mt. 6:33

**"Take my yoke upon you, and learn from me, for I am meek and humble of heart; and you will find rest for your souls. For my yoke is easy, and my burden light."** Mt. 11:29

**"To know Jesus and Him crucified is my philosophy, and there is none higher."** St. Bernard

***From whom do we learn to know, love, and serve God?***

**We learn to know, love, and serve God from Jesus Christ, the Son of God, who teaches us through the Catholic Church.**

*The Preaching of Jesus* Hoffman

When going somewhere for the first time, one has to obtain directions. Thus, when men lost the way to heaven after original sin, Jesus came to give us directions.

For thirty years, He left us the most admirable examples of a holy life. Then for three years He taught in the cities and villages of Palestine—in houses, on mountains, in deserts, and on the boat of Saint Peter, who was a fisherman before becoming an Apostle.

To go to paradise we must travel three roads. On the first are the truths which God has revealed to us and which we must believe. On the second are the commandments which our Lord has given us to obey. On the third we find the holy sacraments and prayer.

In the first place then, we must **believe** all that which Jesus, infallible Truth, has revealed to us through His holy Church; that is, we must believe all the beautiful truths which are contained in the catechism.

There are three guides along the way of faith: the divinely inspired Scripture, sacred Tradition and the infallible teaching of the Church.

**"Thanks be to the Gospel, by means of which we also, who did not see Christ when He came into this world, seem to be with Him when we read His deeds."**

St. Ambrose

*Moses* Ribera-Anders

***What must we do to love God, our neighbor, and ourselves?***

**To love God, our neighbor, and ourselves we must keep the commandments of God and of the Church, and perform the spiritual and corporal works of mercy.**

When God created man, He imprinted His divine law upon his heart. But after the sin of Adam, men became so evil that they no longer clearly heard the voice of God's law in their hearts.

Then God summoned Moses, leader of the Israelites, to the summit of Mount Sinai. There, amid storm clouds, thunder and lightning, He gave Moses His law, written on two stone tablets. In the illustration Moses is showing the tablets of laws to his people.

God's law is contained in the ten commandments. The first three of these concern our duties toward Him: we must love and adore Him, respect His name, avoid those who blaspheme Him, and keep holy the days dedicated to Him.

The other seven commandments concern our duties toward ourselves and our neighbor: we must honor and respect our parents, do good to all, harm no one, be pure in soul and body, respect the possessions of others, and avoid lies, evil thoughts and evil desires.

Then Jesus confirmed and perfected the commandments, and taught us to observe them, not through fear, but with a spirit of filial love.

Let us pray with the prophet:

**"Show me, O Lord, the way of your laws, and I will follow it exactly."**

Ps. 119:33

*Communion in the Catacombs* Vera

***What is actual grace?***

**Actual grace is a supernatural help of God which enlightens our mind and strengthens our will to do good and to avoid evil.**

In the first centuries of its life, the Church was fiercely persecuted by the Roman emperors. It was considered a crime to be a Christian; prisons overflowed with confessors of the Faith and arenas were crowded with martyrs.

Pagans could not understand where the early Christians obtained the fearless strength to profess their Faith at the price of their blood. We, however, know that it was God's grace which gave them the superhuman strength that permitted them to face calmly the most horrible tortures. They acquired grace through fervent prayer and from the sacraments, particularly the Holy Eucharist. Often, in the middle of the night, in subterranean catacombs on the outskirts of Rome, Christians gathered together to celebrate the divine mysteries. They were nourished with the Bread of the strong, and listened to the ardent exhortations of their pastors. At dawn they left, transformed by grace and ready to suffer all things for the love of God.

Grace is that most powerful help which God pours into the souls of those who pray. It strengthens us in the practice of the commandments and in the observance of daily duties. It gives us power to repel the devil's temptations and to resist our nature's bad inclinations. It worthily prepares us for the life of heaven.

The sacraments are channels through which grace flows into the souls of the faithful to enable them to live according to God.

**"I can do all things in him who strengthens me."** Phil. 4:13

*St. Peter, the Martyr* Domenichino-Anderson

***Where do we find the chief truths taught by Jesus Christ through the Catholic Church?***

**We find the chief truths taught by Jesus Christ through the Catholic Church in the Apostles' Creed.**

The truths revealed by God are many, and all are contained in Sacred Scripture and in the Tradition of the Church.

Jesus Christ taught many divine truths in His three years of preaching. Later, His Apostles went throughout the world preaching them to all people.

The Apostles' Creed was compiled very early in the Christian era. This Creed is a summary of the principal articles of faith.

In the Church of old, before being baptized, the neophyte recited his profession of faith, saying the Apostles' Creed. Even today it is the "mark" of a believer. Whoever denies a single article of the Creed denies the Faith. Martyrs have given their lives in defense of the Creed.

St. Peter of Verona, whose martyrdom is shown in the picture, was traveling through the cities of Italy, preaching against the heresies of Waldenses and Albigenses and Patarini—rebels against the Church and upsetters of the social order. These heretics, of course, hated Peter. One day while he was walking from Como to Milan accompanied by a fellow religious, an armed ruffian wounded him. The saint fell, reciting the Creed aloud. He did not succeed in finishing it. As he was dying, he dipped his finger in his own blood and wrote in the sand: **"I believe...."** Wonderful profession of faith!

**"The whole Church which is throughout the whole world possesses one and the same Faith."**

St. Irenaeus

***What is the Church?***

**The Church is the congregation of all baptized persons united in the same true Faith, the same sacrifice, and the same sacraments, under the authority of the Sovereign Pontiff and the bishops in communion with him.**

*The Church* Karl Baumeister

The scene that you see represents the holy Church, which in heaven is made up of angels and saints, and on earth is composed of the faithful guided by their pastors—the Pope, bishops, and priests.

The Church of which we speak is the living Church of souls and hearts, not the building in which we assist at holy Mass. It is a society, or rather, the union of all true Christians. In order to be real Christians, it is necessary to be baptized, to profess the Faith which Jesus has revealed, and to receive the sacraments which Jesus has instituted to sanctify souls. Finally, one must obey the Pope and the bishops, whom the Holy Spirit has made pastors to govern the Church.

The Church is also the Mystical Body of Jesus Christ, of which He is the Head, the Holy Spirit is the Soul and we are the members.

It does not end on earth, but continues in the other life in purgatory and paradise. The Church on earth is **militant,** for it combats the enemies of good; in purgatory it is **suffering,** for there souls are cleansed of every stain or trace of guilt; in heaven it is **triumphant,** for it is glorious with Jesus its Head.

With the most inspiring lyrics De Vere sings of the Church:

**"Hers the kingdom, hers the scepter;**
**Fall, ye nations, at her feet;**
**Hers the truth whose fruit is freedom;**
**Light her yoke, her burden sweet."**

Aubrey De Vere

*Jesus Giving the Keys to Peter* Perugino-Alinari

***Who founded the Church?***
**Jesus Christ founded the Church.**

One day Jesus asked His Apostles what people said about Him. They answered Him: "Some say you are John the Baptist, others say Elijah, still others say you are one of the prophets."

"And you," He said, "who do you think I am?"

St. Peter quickly exclaimed, "You are the Christ, the Son of the living God!" How great Peter's faith was! And to reward him, Jesus answered:

"And I say to you, you are Peter, and upon this rock I will build my Church, and the gates of hell shall not prevail against it. And I will give to you the keys of the kingdom of heaven..." (cf. Mt. 16:13-19).

Thus Jesus promised to found a society that would include all His followers, and He assured Peter that he would be its visible head. This society is the holy Church.

After His glorious resurrection, Jesus fulfilled His promise, conferring upon St. Peter the rights of primacy, jurisdiction and honor in the Church with the words: "Feed my lambs, feed my sheep" (Jn. 21:17).

Jesus founded His Church by gathering about Him His Apostles and His first disciples. Today it extends throughout the world; all of us who have been baptized belong to the true Church of Jesus Christ.

**"The Catholic Church is God's only Church, the single one which in the face of all oppositions, proclaims the whole Truth."** L. Veuillot

*The Basilica of St. Peter* Alinari

***How do we know that the Catholic Church is the one true Church established by Christ?***

**We know that the Catholic Church is the one true Church established by Christ because it alone has the marks of the true Church. By the marks of the Church we mean certain clear signs by which all men can recognize it as the true Church founded by Jesus Christ.**

On Vatican Hill in Rome, on the very spot where St. Peter suffered martyrdom, stands the majestic basilica bearing his name. From all parts of the world the faithful come to visit it—the greatest church of Christianity, a lighthouse of brightness on the globe, an eloquent symbol of the spiritual Church founded on the immovable rock of Peter.

In order to distinguish His Church from all others, Jesus has endowed the Church He founded with four distinct, unmistakable marks: It is **one, holy, catholic** or **universal,** and **apostolic.**

The Church of Jesus Christ is **One** in the whole world. In fact, all its members obey the same Pastor, the Pope; all have the same Faith and receive the same sacraments. It is **Catholic** because it was instituted for all men and is widespread upon the earth. It is **Holy** because everything in the Church is holy and all are called to sanctity. It is **Apostolic** because it was founded upon the Apostles and is governed by the Pope and bishops, who are their successors.

These distinctive marks are found together only in the Catholic Church. Therefore it is the only true Church instituted by Jesus Christ.

**"Rome has become the capital of the Christian world, the watch tower of God's light in the tumult of the world, an immense ship which sails the sea of centuries to the ports of the eternal."** M. Cordovan

*The Lawful Shepherds of the Church* Seitz-Anderson

***What is meant by the authority of the Catholic Church?***

**By the authority of the Catholic Church is meant that the Pope and the bishops, as the lawful successors of the Apostles, have power from Christ Himself to teach, to sanctify, and to govern the faithful in spiritual matters.**

One day Jesus said, "I am the good shepherd, and I know mine, and mine know me. And other sheep I have that are not of this fold. Them also I must bring...and there shall be one fold and one shepherd..." (Jn. 10:14, 16).

The fold of Jesus is the Church and the sheep are all the faithful. However, when Jesus ascended to heaven, He left other shepherds in the world to govern His flock. They were the Apostles, to whom He said, "Go into the whole world and preach the gospel to every creature" (Mk. 16:15). To them Jesus entrusted His authority, His doctrine and His sacraments. The Apostles faithfully transmitted these treasures of faith to their successors, the Pope and the bishops in union with him, who governed the Church down through the centuries.

The beautiful illustration represents the Catholic hierarchy, who constitute the teaching Church entrusted with the task of teaching and governing the faithful.

The Pope and bishops are legitimate pastors because they are the successors of the Apostles. The Pope governs the whole Church. The bishops govern their dioceses and are represented by the pastors and priests in each parish.

**"Brothers," exhorts St. Paul, "obey your superiors, and be subject to them, for they keep watch as having to render an account of your souls."**

Heb. 13:17

***Did Christ intend that the special power of chief teacher and ruler of the entire Church should be exercised by St. Peter alone?***

**Christ did not intend that the special power of chief teacher and ruler of the entire Church should be exercised by St. Peter alone, but intended that this power should be passed down to his Successor, the Pope, the Bishop of Rome, who is the Vicar of Christ on earth and the visible head of the Church.**

*His Holiness, Pope John Paul II*

St. Peter was the first Vicar of Jesus Christ. A vicar is one who either represents or substitutes for another person. The Pope represents Jesus Christ and he is thus His Vicar. St. Catherine of Siena called him: "the Sweet Christ on earth."

After Pentecost, St. Peter went to preach the Gospel in Rome, the great capital of the world's largest empire. He was the first Bishop of Rome. When, during the reign of the Emperor Nero, St. Peter was martyred on Vatican Hill, crucified head downward, St. Linus succeeded him in the government of the Church, and others have succeeded him until this very day. All the supreme Pontiffs are successors of St. Peter.

The true Head of the Church is Jesus, who founded it, but after His ascension into heaven He became its **invisible Head.** The Pope represents Jesus and is the **visible head** of the whole Church.

**"I follow no one as chief save Christ, but I am joined in communion with your blessedness, that is, with the See of Peter. Upon that rock I know the Church is built."**

St. Jerome to Pope Damasus

**"May this be your most glorious motto: Catholics with the Pope!"**

St. John Bosco

*Faith and Religion in the Christian School* Seitz-Anderson

***What is meant by the infallibility of the Catholic Church?***

**By the infallibility of the Catholic Church is meant that the Church, by the special assistance of the Holy Spirit, cannot err when it teaches or believes a doctrine of faith or morals.**

Before leaving this earth Jesus Christ promised His disciples that He would not leave them orphans: **"Behold I am with you all days, even unto the consummation of the world"** (Mt. 28:20). This divine promise is realized in the Sacrament of the Holy Eucharist and in the Holy Spirit's assistance to the Church so that it may teach without error.

Thus the Church in the exercise of its solemn and ordinary Magisterium has the unspeakably great prerogative of infallibility and freedom from error since: "He will give you another Advocate to dwell with you forever, the Spirit of truth" (Jn. 14:16, 17).

Observe with what realistic imagery the artist has personified the Magisterium of the Catholic Church. It is portrayed by a woman whose gaze is steady and clear, and upon whose shining forehead God's light is reflected. In her right hand she holds the flame of the Gospel, and in her left, an olive branch, the symbol of the peace which springs only from the truth. The angels around her are holding the Sacred Scriptures—font of truth—and the commandments of God and the commandments of the Church—safe norms of eternal life.

Jesus Christ assured Peter of infallibility with these words:

**"Simon, Simon, behold Satan has desired to have you, that he may sift you as wheat. But I have prayed for you, that your faith may not fail; and do you, when once you have turned again, strengthen your brethren."**

Lk. 22:31, 32

***When is the Church's teaching infallible?***

**The Church teaches infallibly when it teaches or defines, through the Pope alone, as the teacher of all Christians, or through the Pope and the bishops, a doctrine of faith or morals to be held by all the faithful.**

*The Proclamation of the Dogma of the Immaculate Conception* Podesti-Anderson

On December 8, 1854, the angelic Pope Pius IX solemnly defined the dogma of the Immaculate Conception. This incomparable gem of the Virgin Mary, this truth alluded to in the Old Testament, contained implicitly in the Gospels, strenuously defended and lovingly illustrated by many Doctors of the Church, was finally confirmed by the seal of infallibility amid the joy of all the faithful. It was a cloudy winter morning; but at the moment when the Pontiff, standing before his throne, solemnly proclaimed the Immaculate Conception of Mary a dogma of Faith, a luminous ray burst through the clouds and rested upon the forehead of the Supreme Pontiff, Pius IX.

Four years later, the Blessed Virgin appeared to Bernadette at Lourdes, confirming the words of the Supreme Pontiff by saying: "I am the Immaculate Conception."

An Ecumenical Council of the Catholic Episcopacy may teach infallibly when convened and solemnly approved by the Pope, just as the Pope is infallible by himself, when as shepherd and teacher of all Christians, he defines doctrines concerning faith and morals.

**"The Roman Pontiff is Peter living throughout the ages."** M. Cordovan

*The Dogma of the Immaculate Conception* Podesti-Anderson

***When is the Church's teaching infallible?***

**The Church teaches infallibly when it teaches or defines, through the Pope alone, as the teacher of every Christian, or through the Pope and the bishops, a doctrine of faith or morals to be held by all the faithful.**

The picture represents the general assembly of bishops, abbots and illustrious theologians held at Rome in 1854 for the definition of the dogma of the Immaculate Conception.

The ordinary Magisterium is continually exercised by the Church especially by preaching. The solemn Magisterium is exercised by the Church only rarely by formal and authentic definitions of councils or Popes. An ecumenical council is the general assembly of the Catholic episcopacy with the Roman Pontiff or one of his representatives presiding. What solemnity! The council of the Pope and bishops in union with him is a living image of that unity by which the Church victoriously overcomes every insidious error and false doctrine.

The Pope and bishops are the teachers and shepherds of Christianity. To them is granted the sacred trust of supernatural revelation contained in Sacred Scripture and Tradition. Only the teaching Church has the right to interpret and explain, as to it alone is reserved the task of judging every question regarding faith, morals, and worship.

The Pope and bishops, as successors of the Apostles, continue the mission of Jesus in the world by remaining faithful to the divine order, **"Go, therefore, and make disciples of all nations, baptizing them and teaching them to observe all that I have commanded you."** Mt. 28:19

***What is a supernatural mystery?***

**A supernatural mystery is a truth which we cannot fully understand, but which we firmly believe because we have God's word for it.**

In the Creed we make a profession of many truths of the Christian Faith. Some of them are "mysteries," that is, truths that our mind cannot succeed in understanding, but which we believe on the authority of God revealing them, who can neither deceive nor be deceived.

*The Blessed Trinity* M. Albertinelli-Alinari

Of the mysteries professed in the Creed, there are two principal ones, because they are the foundation for all the other truths of our holy religion. They are:

The unity and Trinity of God.

The Incarnation, passion and death of our Lord Jesus Christ.

The picture wonderfully explains these two mysteries. In it, we see the eternal Father, the first Person of the Blessed Trinity, holding up the pierced body of Jesus Christ, the second Person, and hovering between them, the Dove, which represents the Holy Spirit, the third Person.

The lifeless body of Jesus, His thorn-crowned head, the nail marks in His hands and feet, the bleeding wound in His side, the instruments of the passion, all remind us that the Son of God was made man, suffered and died on the cross in order to redeem us from our sins.

We cannot understand this mystery; we **believe** it. Dante warns:

**"Full mad is he who with mere reason poses,**
**to penetrate that infinite quandry,**
**which Persons Three in Nature One discloses."** Purg. C. 3:36

*The Discovery of the Cross* Tiepolo-Anderson

***Why do we make the Sign of the Cross?***

**We make the Sign of the Cross to express two important mysteries of the Christian religion, the Blessed Trinity and the redemption.**

The cross is the distinctive sign of a Christian. Just as there are external signs to express an idea, emotion, or event, so too, there is an external sign to manifest the Christian Faith and the greatest event in history: this sign is **the Sign of the Cross.**

For centuries the cross has triumphed in the world. Once it was a symbol of ignominy, but now it is a promise of victory. The cross stands out in the heavens on mountain peaks, on church steeples, on tabernacles and on the tombs of our beloved dead. The Emperor Constantine emblazoned it on his imperial standard and shields, and with this sign, as he had been promised, he won the striking victory over his rival.

In the words used in the Sign of the Cross, we express faith in the unity and Trinity of God; and with the form of the cross which we make on ourselves we recall the Incarnation, passion and death of our Lord Jesus Christ.

Observe the mother of Constantine, St. Helena, who had the wonderful fortune of finding the true cross of Jesus on Mount Calvary after it had been lost for centuries, thus giving it back to the Church as a most precious relic.

**"Let us not be ashamed of the cross of Christ; but do openly seal it upon your forehead, that the devils may behold the royal sign and flee trembling far away."**

St. Cyril of Jerusalem

***How are the mysteries of the Blessed Trinity and the redemption expressed by the Sign of the Cross?***

**When we say "In the name," we express the truth that there is only one God; when we say "of the Father, and of the Son, and of the Holy Spirit," we express the truth that there are three distinct Persons in God; and when we make the form of the cross on ourselves, we express the truth that the Son of God made man redeemed us by His death on the cross.**

*The Sign of the Cross* De Chirico-Anderson

There is no more gentle or delicate gesture on earth than that of a mother joining her child's hands in the act of prayer. All Christian mothers make this gesture of faith over and over again and teach it to their little ones.

Souls with a living faith make the Sign of the Cross with seriousness and devotion. St. Bernadette Soubirous learned from Mary Immaculate to make the Sign of the Cross with deep piety and recollection.

A Christian sanctifies all his actions with the Sign of the Cross. Tertullian wrote, "We make the Sign of the Cross before travel and rest, when sitting at table and rising from it, at the beginning and end of each day, in dangers of soul and body."

It is most helpful to make the Sign of the Cross often and devoutly, for it is an external act of faith, it revives the virtue of faith in us, it conquers human pride and temptations, and it wins God's graces for us.

**"This sign of the passion is displayed and made manifest against the devil if you make it in faith, not in order that you may be seen by men, but by your knowledge putting it forward as a shield."** St. Hippolytus

**Free us, O Lord, from our enemies through the Sign of the Cross.**

Liturgy

*Jacob's Dream* Alinari

***Which are the chief creatures of God?***
**The chief creatures of God are angels and men.**

Observe Jacob's vision in the illustration. He was fleeing from home out of fear of his brother, Esau, whose birthright and paternal blessing he had extorted. At last, feeling tired, he lay down on the ground and fell asleep. In a dream he saw a ladder extending from earth to heaven as far as God; many angels were ascending and descending it.

God granted this vision to Jacob to assure him of His divine help. The angels, in fact, descend to earth bringing the aid and counsel of Almighty God to men, and they ascend to heaven with man's prayers to God.

Angels and men are God's chief creatures.

Man is a noble creature, composed of body and soul. His soul is an immortal spirit. Angels are more perfect spirits, superior to man's soul. They are the highest of God's creatures.

**"Whenever we look abroad, we are reminded of those most gracious and holy beings, the angels, servants of the Holiest, who deign to minister to the heirs of salvation."** Cardinal Newman

**"Make yourself familiar with the angels, and behold them frequently in spirit; for without being seen, they are present with you."**
St. Francis de Sales

***What is a spirit?***

**A spirit is a being that has understanding and free will, but no body, and will never die.**

***What are angels?***

**Angels are created spirits, without bodies, having understanding and free will.**

*The Martyrdom of St. Justin (Detail)* Veronese-Alinari

Celestial spirits generally appear in the form of splendid youths, warriors and messengers of the Lord. God permits them to appear under human form so that man may perceive their presence and understand their mission.

To aid our imagination, artists depict angels in the form of children and gracious young people, adorned with splendor, innocence and sanctity. They represent them as heavenly beings with wings to indicate the promptness with which they execute God's wishes.

Behold how Paul Veronese succeeded in representing a group of celestial spirits. Immersed in a sea of divine light, bands of angels are singing hosannas to the Lord in celestial harmonies; others are winging their way to earth with palm branches, crowns, wreaths and lilies as though to encourage men to fight fearlessly against evil.

Pure spirits have incomparable beauty in God's eyes, for they are rich in grace and sanctity; they are endowed with perfect intelligence; they have a power that is superior to that of any other created strength. They are innumerable—more, maintains St. Thomas, than all material creatures taken together. What a splendid and wondrous army! They are divided into nine choirs: angels, archangels, principalities, powers, virtues, dominations, thrones, cherubim and seraphim.

**"O you angels of the Lord, bless the Lord!"** Dn. 3:58

*The Guardian Angel* Domenichino-Anderson

***What gifts did God bestow on the angels when He created them?***

**When God created the angels He bestowed on them great wisdom, power, and holiness.**

***How do the good angels help us?***

**The good angels help us by praying for us, by acting as messengers from God to us, and by serving as our guardian angels.**

God created numberless bands of angels to constitute His court of honor in heaven and to be His **ministers,** to serve Him in various ways. Often He sends them to manifest His will to men, as He did on the occasions of the annunciation, the nativity of Christ, and the resurrection.

In heaven, the angels see, love, and adore God.

The angels are also our guardians. We are entrusted from the day of our birth to the guidance of an angel who never abandons us, and goes everywhere with us to protect us from harm and to inspire us to do good.

Let us always honor our good angel, be grateful to him, and love him. Let us listen to him, and invoke him often in dangers and when the devil tempts us to sin.

**"See, I am sending an angel before you, to guard you on the way.... Be attentive to him and heed his voice."** Ex. 23:20-21

**"The servants of Christ are protected by invisible rather than visible beings. But if these guard you, they do so because they have been summoned by your prayers."** St. Ambrose

***Did all the angels remain faithful to God?***

**Not all the angels remained faithful to God; some of them sinned.**

***What happened to the angels who did not remain faithful to God?***

**The angels who did not remain faithful to God were cast into hell, and these are called bad angels, or devils.**

*St. Michael the Archangel* Guido Reni-Anderson

Once Lucifer was the most beautiful angel in paradise, but he became proud, dared to rebel against God and drew many other rebellious angels with him. St. Michael and all the faithful angels rose to combat him. Thus, Lucifer and his followers were driven from paradise and hurled into hell. Now we call them devils.

They, too, like the angels, are pure spirits without a body. They are God's enemies, who hate Him and envy us because we are destined by our Lord to occupy the places which they abandoned in heaven!

Not being able to take revenge on God, they try in every way to harm us, disturbing our mind with evil thoughts, and our heart with bad affections. They thus incite us to sin, which is rebellion against God.

We must never listen to the devil's insinuations, but should drive them away quickly by calling upon the help of our guardian angel. The saints say that the devil is like a dog on a leash: he barks a great deal, but only bites those who go near him.

**"The devil tempts all the servants of God. Those who are strong in the faith resist him and he goes away from them, because he cannot find entrance. So, he goes then to the empty, and finding an entrance, he goes into them. Thus he accomplishes in them whatever he pleases and makes them his slaves."**

Shepherd of Hermas

*The Creation of Woman* Dorè-Garzanti

***What is man?***

**Man is a creature composed of body and soul, and made to the image and likeness of God.**

***How is the soul like God?***

**The soul is like God because it is a spirit having understanding and free will, and is destined to live forever.**

After having created heaven and earth, light and all things, God said, **"Let us make man to our image and likeness"** (Gn. 1:26).

He formed man of the slime of the earth and breathed into his face the breath of life and man became a living being. Then He sent a deep sleep upon the man, Adam. He took one of his ribs, and with it made Eve, the first woman and mother of the human race.

Man and woman are composed of a spiritual soul and an earthly body. The soul, the most noble part of man, makes him resemble God more than any other creature of the earth.

Adam and Eve were happy in the terrestrial paradise until they abused their liberty and disobeyed God by eating the forbidden fruit.

What a great gift the soul is: We should thank the Lord for having made us capable of knowing Him, loving Him and serving Him.

**"Despise the flesh, for it passes away; be solicitous for your soul which will never die."** St. Basil

***Do human souls live forever?***

**Because they are spirits, human souls live forever.**

Man's soul is **spiritual**; and because it is spiritual, it is **independent** of the body, with which it is often in opposition. In fact, how many times the body enjoys pleasure while the soul experiences the sadness of death!

Since the soul is spiritual, simple and independent of the body, it cannot be destroyed by death.

The property of immortality belongs to the human soul as a spiritual substance.

*The Martyrdom of St. Felicitas* Giorgio Berto-Brogi

The illustration represents St. Felicitas, a noble Roman matron of the second century. The energetic movement of her arms shows that she was a strong woman; her dignified expression portrays the determined strength of her faith. A widow with seven children, she educated them as only a fervent Christian mother can, and when accused before the emperor, she and her children declared themselves ready to give their lives for Christ. With heroic fortitude, St. Felicitas watched each of her children being martyred. "Courage!" she cried, as they were tortured by hooks and pierced by the sword, "Courage!" And all of them, including the mother, received the palm of martyrdom.

**"Death shall be no more, but never-failing health; no anxiety, but blessed delight, and a society sweet and glorious."** Imitation of Christ

**"Little does passing time matter to a soul which aspires to eternity, and which only takes notice of perishing moments in order to pass by them into immortal life."** St. Francis de Sales

*The Martyrdom of Sts. Mark and Marcellinus* Veronese-Anderson

***For what do we pray when we say "and lead us not into temptation"?***

**When we say "and lead us not into temptation," we pray that God will always give us the grace to overcome temptations to sin which come to us from the world, the flesh, and the devil.**

In this striking picture, Paul Veronese shows us the martyrdom of Sts. Mark and Marcellinus, two famous Roman brothers. The captain clutching the banner and pointing to heaven is St. Sebastian.

Accused of being Christians, Mark and Marcellinus were thrown into prison, condemned to death by beheading. Their parents, who were still pagans, had the execution deferred for a month, for they hoped to make them deny their Faith. However, the two heroes remained faithful to the religion of Christ, although deeply moved by their family's tears.

Having heard that the faith of Mark and Marcellinus was being tried, St. Sebastian, who was then captain of the praetorian guard and very dear to the Emperor Diocletian, hurried to the prison. In glowing terms, he spoke of Christ, of the immeasurable value of the soul, and of heaven. So inflamed were his words that not only was the faith of the two men strengthened but their parents were converted and crowned their lives with martyrdom, too. Today they are honored as saints.

What would it have availed Mark and Marcellinus had they saved their lives but lost their souls? The soul is our better part, the most precious treasure we possess. By saving it we will be eternally happy; otherwise we will have lost all!

The Divine Master warns, **"For what does it profit a man, if he gain the whole world, but suffer the loss of his own soul? Or what will a man give in exchange for his soul?"** Mt. 16:26

***How was the Son of God made man?***

**The Son of God was conceived and made man by the power of the Holy Spirit in the womb of the Blessed Virgin Mary.**

The Archangel Gabriel entered the humble home in which the Virgin Mary was praying, and said to her:

"Hail, full of grace, the Lord is with you.... Behold you shall bring forth a son; and you shall call his name Jesus. He shall be called the Son of the Most High, and he shall be king forever."

And Mary said to the angel: "How shall this happen, since I do not know man?"

The angel answered: "The Holy Spirit shall come upon you, and the power of the Most High shall overshadow you; and therefore the Holy One to be born shall be called the Son of God."

*The Annunciation* Murillo-Anderson

Then Mary answered: "Behold the handmaid of the Lord; be it done to me according to your word" (Lk. 1:26-38).

At that instant the great mystery of the Incarnation was accomplished and Mary became the Mother of the Son of God.

The Son of God became man by taking to Himself a body and soul like ours, in the most pure womb of the Virgin Mary by the power of the Holy Spirit.

**"And the Word was made flesh, and dwelt among us. And we saw his glory—glory as of the only-begotten of the Father—full of grace and of truth."** Jn. 1:14

**"To know Jesus and Him crucified is my philosophy, and there is none higher."** St. Bernard

*The Holy Family* Albani-Anderson

***What is meant by the Incarnation?***

**By the Incarnation is meant that the Son of God, retaining His divine nature, took to Himself a human nature, that is, a body and soul like ours.**

By becoming man, the Son of God did not cease to be God. Being God, He is eternal; He always was and always will be.

At the moment of the Incarnation, the second Person of the Blessed Trinity assumed a human nature, that is, He united to His divine Person a body, taken from Mary's most pure womb, and a soul.

Thus Jesus Christ is both God and man.

The beautiful picture represents the Holy Family: Jesus, Mary, and Joseph. As man, Jesus is like us in all things, except sin. Yet, as God, He is equal in everything to the Father and the Holy Spirit, together with whom He forms the Blessed Trinity.

Let us adore the Son of God, who became the Son of Mary, and our Brother, in order to show us His love and to win the entire affection of our hearts.

**"We hope in the living God, who is the Savior of all men, especially of believers."**

1 Tm. 4:10

**"You are sweet, Jesus, You are my Creator; in You, O Savior, will I be justified."**

Byzantine Triodion

***When was the Son of God conceived and made man?***

**The Son of God was conceived and made man on Annunciation Day, the day on which the Angel Gabriel announced to the Blessed Virgin Mary that she was to be the Mother of God.**

There exist few artists who have not attempted to portray on canvas or in marble the supremely beautiful Mother of God.

Contemplate the picture in which Dolci, with soft colors, has depicted the Virgin Mary holding her divine Son. What tenderness and devotion! Jesus was Mary's Son, but He was also her God, and all the loving attention the young Mother lavished on her Child was ardent, continual prayer.

*Madonna with the Infant Jesus* Dolci-Alinari

Having preordained from all eternity that the Word of the Father would be made man in order to redeem men, the Blessed Trinity chose a Mother for Him and endowed her with privileges and graces that she might be a worthy tabernacle for the Son of God.

Mary is truly the Mother of God. She conceived Him in her womb, she gave Him birth, she nourished Him, educated Him and gave Him all the care that the tenderest mother could give to her child. Her heart had to be His compensation for all the praises of the angels, and her beauty had to surpass the marvels of heaven.

You are all beautiful and immaculate, O Virgin Mother, because on your face shines the splendor of your divine Son!

**"Mary, by the very fact that she brought forth the Redeemer of the human race, is also in a manner the most tender mother of us all, whom Christ our Lord deigned to have as His brothers."** Pope Pius XI

*St. Joseph's Dream* Guercino-Anderson

***Is St. Joseph the father of Jesus Christ?***

**Jesus Christ had no human father, but St. Joseph was the spouse of the Blessed Virgin Mary and the guardian, or foster-father, of Christ.**

In the picture, St. Joseph, the carpenter of Nazareth, is shown resting. In his sleep, the angel is gently announcing to him that his most holy bride has been chosen to be the Mother of God and that the Savior of the world will soon be born of her.

Jesus had only one true Father, His eternal Father in heaven. St. Joseph was His foster father, and for this reason, Jesus was called the son of the carpenter.

Jesus honored Joseph with the sweet name of father. In fact, the eternal Father had conferred paternal authority on St. Joseph by entrusting to his care His most precious treasure, His divine Son, so that he might provide for Him with a father's love.

**"Joseph was a prudent and faithful servant, whom the Lord placed beside Mary to be her protector, the nourisher of His human body, and the most trusty assistant on earth in His great design."** St. Bernard

**"Though you have recourse to many saints as your intercessors, go especially to St. Joseph, for he has great power with God."**

St. Teresa of Jesus

*The Birth of Jesus* Murillo-Alinari

***When was Christ born?***

**Christ was born of the Blessed Virgin Mary on Christmas Day in Bethlehem, more than nineteen hundred years ago.**

The manger scene is one of the most typical and moving expressions of Christian piety. Note how beautifully Murillo has depicted the Infant Jesus, the Blessed Virgin, St. Joseph, and the humble shepherds.

Jesus was born in Bethlehem, of Palestine, in a poor stable, and was placed by His holy Mother in a manger. The night was cold and dark, but a brilliant light shone in the darkness, and angels appeared, singing: **"Glory to God in the highest; and on earth peace among men of good will"** (Lk. 2:14).

In the nearby fields, shepherds were watching their sheep when an angel invited them to go seek the Infant. The shepherds hastened to the stable. Prostrating themselves before Jesus in adoration, they offered Him their gifts. A wondrous star also appeared in the heavens of the East. The Magi saw it, and left their distant homes to follow it to Bethlehem. In Bethlehem, the star stood over the place where the Child was. Rejoicing, the Magi entered the house and worshiped the holy Infant. Then, opening their treasures, they offered Him gold, frankincense and myrrh.

**"One difference between Christ and other men is this: they do not choose when to be born, but He, the Lord and Maker of history, chose His time, His birthplace, and His Mother."** St. Thomas Aquinas

*The Holy Family* Gagliardi-Alinari

***How can our most ordinary actions merit a heavenly reward?***

**We can make our most ordinary actions merit a heavenly reward by doing them well for the love of God and by keeping ourselves in the state of grace.**

Jesus was a little laborer. In the illustration, He is in St. Joseph's small shop learning the carpenter's trade. St. Joseph and the Blessed Virgin, too, worked, for they were poor and earned their daily bread by the sweat of their brow.

Jesus was the Son of God, Lord of the universe! Nevertheless, to teach us to be humble and not to attach our hearts to the wealth, comforts and pleasures of life, He willed to be a modest workingman and to live in obscurity for thirty years.

One is not made happy by enjoyment, money and amusements, but rather by imitation of Jesus in charity, humility, and honest labor. Let us always remember His invitation: **"Learn from me, for I am meek and humble of heart!"** (Mt. 11:29)

Christ teaches us what real blessedness is:

> **"Blessed are the poor in spirit, for theirs is the kingdom of heaven.**
> **Blessed are the meek, for they shall possess the earth.**
> **Blessed are they who mourn, for they shall be comforted.**
> **Blessed are they who hunger and thirst for justice, for they shall be satisfied."**
>
> cf. Mt. 5:1-7

**"It is to the humble-minded that Christ belongs. He did not, for all His power, come clothed in boastful pomp and arrogant pride, but in a humble frame of mind."**

Pope St. Clement I

*The Burial of Jesus* Ciseri-Alinari

***What were the chief sufferings of Christ?***

**The chief sufferings of Christ were His bitter agony of soul, His bloody sweat, His cruel scourging, His crowning with thorns, His crucifixion, and His death on the cross.**

Jesus, Goodness itself, did good to all. He cured the sick, He brought the dead back to life, and He taught everyone the way to heaven.

His enemies, fiercely jealous of His fame, sought to kill Him. With a kiss, the traitor Judas betrayed Him into their hands. Jesus was bound, insulted, scourged and crowned with thorns. Then, having been condemned to death by Pilate, He was given a cross to carry to Calvary, where He was crucified between two thieves. The Savior hung for three hours on the cross in great agony. Yet He mercifully forgave His crucifiers. At last, He bowed His head and gave up His spirit, whereupon a soldier took a lance and pierced His heart.

Followers of Jesus came then and, with the Sorrowful Virgin and the holy women, they brought the body of the Redeemer away to its burial.

Jesus was God and man. But God can neither suffer nor die. Only man, who has a body composed of matter, of cells and living tissues, must one day see it dissolve and return to the earth from which it came. Thus, it was only as man that Jesus died; He, the Son of God, had become man for the very purpose of being able to suffer and die for us.

**"The cross of Christ is the true ground and chief cause of Christian hope."**

Pope St. Leo I

*The Resurrection* Benvenuti-Alinari

***When did Christ rise from the dead?***

**Christ rose from the dead, glorious and immortal, on Easter Sunday, the third day after His death.**

The day on which Jesus died is known as Good Friday.

While His body was lying in the sepulcher, Jesus' soul descended to Limbo, where the souls of the just were awaiting the time when the gates of heaven would be reopened. Jesus consoled these souls and assured them of their entrance into heaven on the day of His ascension. Jesus had often foretold His resurrection and He almost never spoke of His passion to His disciples without alluding to the resurrection. Even His enemies knew of His prediction, and for this reason they sealed the sepulcher and placed guards to watch it.

On the morning of the third day, Sunday, there was a great earthquake. Jesus rose from the dead, triumphant and glorious, by His own almighty power.

The resurrection is the greatest and most important of Christ's miracles. This miracle by itself alone proves that He is God. The entire Church celebrates Easter Sunday in memory of Christ's glorious resurrection.

**"In order that I might have the hope of resurrecting, You, O my God, came back to life before me, so that, where You preceded me, I may hope to follow You."**

St. Augustine

***When did Christ ascend into heaven?***

**Christ ascended, body and soul, into heaven on ascension day, forty days after His resurrection.**

After the resurrection, Jesus remained on earth for forty days, to prove that He had truly risen from the dead, and to complete the instruction of the Apostles. He appeared many times to His disciples. He walked, talked and even ate with them, so that they might not have any doubt as to the great miracle. Only Thomas would not believe it, until Jesus bade him put his finger into the wounds of His hands and side.

*The Ascension* Murione-Alinari

After forty days, Jesus led His Apostles and disciples to the Mount of Olives. There He blessed them, commanded them to preach the Gospel to all nations, and promised to be with them all days, even unto the end of the world. Then He was lifted up before their eyes and was carried up into heaven.

Jesus ascended into heaven, body and soul. Together with the holy souls freed from Limbo, He entered paradise in triumph. In heaven, even as man, He sits at the right hand of the Father. He reigns gloriously in heaven and on earth, and His reign will never come to an end.

The paradise into which Jesus entered triumphantly is the reward promised to all faithful souls.

The Apostle Paul wrote on the eve of his martyrdom: **"I have fought the good fight, I have finished the course, I have kept the faith. For the rest, there is laid up for me a crown of justice, which the Lord, the just Judge, will give to me in that day; yet not to me only, but also to those who love his coming."**

2 Tm. 4:7-8

*The Triumph of the Eucharist* Raffaello-Anderson

***Is Jesus Christ now only in heaven?***

**Jesus Christ now is not only in heaven but as God, He is everywhere, and as God and man, He is in heaven and in the Blessed Sacrament of the altar.**

When Jesus ascended into heaven, He did not leave His followers alone in the world, like a departed parent leaving orphaned children. "I will not leave you orphans," He had said (Jn. 14:18). Because of His love for us, He told us: "I am with you all days, even to the consummation of the world" (Mt. 28:20). And He has remained with us in the most holy Sacrament of the Eucharist.

The picture which Raphael's splendid art created gathers heaven and earth about the sacred Host in a wonderful harmony of faith and love.

As God, Jesus is everywhere. As God and man, however, He is in heaven with the eternal Father, the Holy Spirit, the angels, and the saints, and on earth in the Holy Eucharist.

Jesus is in every consecrated Host of the world, and when we go to Holy Communion we receive the Body, Blood, Soul and Divinity of our Savior into our hearts.

The world does not see Him, but we see Him with the eyes of faith; we hear Him speak to our souls and we feel His grace and love.

**"When you see the sacred Host, say to yourself: This is that Body which was once covered with blood and pierced by a lance.... This Body He gave to us to keep and to eat, as a mark of His intense love."** St. John Chrysostom

**"My soul desires to receive Your Body; my heart longs to unite itself to You. Give Yourself to me and it will suffice me; for outside of You no consolation satisfies me. Therefore, I must approach You often, and receive You to restore health to my soul."** The Imitation of Christ

***Will Jesus Christ ever return visibly to this earth?***

**Jesus Christ will return visibly to this earth at the end of the world to judge all men, that is, everyone who has ever lived in this world.**

*The Universal Judgment* Benvenuti-Alinari

On ascension day, as Jesus rose into the heavens, the Apostles stood looking up in utter amazement. Two angels appeared to them and said: "Men of Galilee, why do you stand looking up to heaven? This Jesus who has been taken up from you into heaven, shall come in the same way as you have seen him going up to heaven" (Acts 1:11). Therefore, Jesus will again return to this earth, at the end of the world. He will come in the full splendor of His glory to judge all men, the just and the wicked, who will be gathered together from the ends of the earth. This judgment which will be passed on all men immediately after the general resurrection is called the general judgment.

The **general judgment** is a subject which has inspired many great artists—including Benvenuti, whose work appears here—to create works striking for contrasts of color, rich detail, and dramatic power.

The divine Judge will say to the good: "Come, blessed of my Father, take possession of the kingdom prepared for you from the foundation of the world." To the evil He will say rather: "Depart from me, accursed ones, into the everlasting fire which was prepared for the devil and his angels" (Mt. 25:34, 41).

Then the good will jubilantly enter into heaven, while the wicked will be cast into hell, condemned to endless excruciating torment.

**"But the day of the Lord will come as a thief; at that time the heavens will pass away with great violence, and the elements will be dissolved with heat, and the earth, and the works that are in it, will be burned up."**

2 Pt. 3:10

*Particular Judgment* Jozel Janssens-Ed. Die Christliche Kunst

***Will Jesus Christ wait until the end of the world to judge us?***

**Jesus Christ will not wait until the end of the world to judge us; He will judge each soul immediately after death.**

***What is the judgment called which will be passed on each one of us immediately after death?***

**The judgment which will be passed on each one of us immediately after death is called the particular judgment.**

As soon as a person dies, his soul appears before God to render an account of his entire life: of every thought, word, deed, and omission. St. Paul warns: **"It is appointed unto men to die once, but after this comes the judgment"** (Heb. 9:27).

Observe the picture. The angel of death is going about gathering his harvest. The just are the good wheat; the wicked are the weeds. A soul in the state of grace is presenting itself to the Lord with the lamp of faith to receive its reward. A mortally sinful soul, instead, is being cast by the angel of justice into hell.

At the particular judgment, the sentence will be passed by Jesus Christ; it will be final and will be ratified at the general judgment.

The rewards or punishments appointed for men after the particular judgment are heaven, purgatory, or hell. He who dies in his **baptismal innocence,** or after having fully satisfied for all the sins he committed, will go at once to **heaven.** He who dies in the state of grace, but is in venial sin, or has not fully satisfied for the temporal punishment due his forgiven sins, will go for a time to **purgatory.** He who dies in **mortal sin,** even if only with one single unrepented mortal sin, will go at once to **hell.**

**"He who loves God with his whole heart neither fears death, nor punishment, nor judgment, nor hell; because perfect love gives certain access to God."**

The Imitation of Christ

*The Dead Rise From the Sea* — Lord Lighton-Anderson

***What is the judgment called which will be passed on all men immediately after the general resurrection?***

**The judgment which will be passed on all men immediately after the general resurrection is called the general judgment.**

***What is meant by "the resurrection of the body"?***

**By "the resurrection of the body" is meant that at the end of the world the bodies of all men will rise from the earth and be united again to their souls, nevermore to be separated.**

Sanctified by Baptism, our bodies have become temples of the Lord. Therefore, after death, they will not remain forever in the dark bosom of the earth. At the end of the world, at the sound of the trumpet, the dead will awake. The bodies of all men will rise from graves the world over and from the depths of the sea to be united again to their souls, nevermore to be separated.

The bodies of the just will be impassible, bright, agile and subtle. They will no longer be subject to suffering; they will be radiant with glory; they will be able to travel with the quickness of thought; they will be able to penetrate material substances.

The bodies of the wicked, instead, will be ugly, deformed, and frightening.

The good will ascend to heaven to enjoy their eternal reward, whereas the wicked will fall headlong into hell, to suffer eternal punishment in their bodies, also.

The thought of the general judgment made saints tremble, for they already heard in their souls the echo of the last trumpet. Let us repeat with them the sweet prayer:

**O Jesus, be not my Judge, but my Savior!**

*Eternal Life* Conti

***What is meant by "eternal life"?***

**By "eternal life" is meant that there will be another existence after this present life, and in it the just will be happy for all eternity in heaven, and the reprobate will be punished for all eternity in hell.**

After the last judgment, when each soul will have received the reward or punishment deserved, a life without change or end will begin in heaven and in hell. The hands of time's clock will turn no more.

Eternal life! Everyone in heaven will be happy forever, everyone in hell will be eternally tormented. In heaven, only joy; in hell, only despair.

On the gates of God's kingdom will be written: To be happy always, never to suffer! On the gates of hell will be written: To suffer always, never to be happy!

There will never be a tomorrow. It will always be today, an endless day.

In heaven, souls will have true life, true happiness in seeing God, loving Him, and being united to Him.

In hell, on the other hand, souls will not be able to see and love God, and thus they will not have life, only eternal death.

Let us often meditate on these fundamental truths: One God! One soul! One eternity!

The Apostle exhorts us to look at **"the things that are not seen. For the things that are seen are temporal, but the things that are not seen are eternal."** 2 Cor. 4:18

PART II

# CHRISTIAN MORALITY

***Which are the commandments of God?***

**The commandments of God are these ten:**

1. **I am the Lord thy God; thou shalt not have strange gods before me.**
2. **Thou shalt not take the name of the Lord thy God in vain.**
3. **Remember thou keep holy the Lord's day.**
4. **Honor thy father and thy mother.**
5. **Thou shalt not kill.**
6. **Thou shalt not commit adultery.**
7. **Thou shalt not steal.**
8. **Thou shalt not bear false witness against thy neighbor.**
9. **Thou shalt not covet thy neighbor's wife.**
10. **Thou shalt not covet thy neighbor's goods.**

The illustration depicts Moses descending from Sinai with the two tablets of stone given him by God, on which are carved the ten commandments. To the people awaiting him with outstretched arms he presents these commandments not as a yoke but as a precious gift from God.

As a wise Lawgiver, God has prescribed a norm and moral guide for His creatures, that they may understand and accomplish good and avoid evil. If we faithfully follow this guide, it will lead us to salvation.

In the New Testament, our Lord Jesus Christ did not abolish the ten commandments; rather, He confirmed and explained them. He taught us to practice them out of love and in view of the heavenly reward.

**"If you love me, keep my commandments."**

Jn. 14:15

*Moses with the Tablets of Laws* Dorè-Garzanti

*Abel's Murder* Benvenuti-Alinari

***Is it always a mortal sin to violate a commandment of God?***

**To violate deliberately even one commandment of God in a serious matter is a mortal sin.**

A boy displeases his father if he disobeys him; he offends him because he lacks respect for him. The ten commandments are our heavenly Father's orders; those who do not keep them, who violate even only one, disobey God, and offend Him.

Whoever offends God commits sin and deserves punishment. The severity of the punishment depends on the gravity of the offense given to God.

The child who steals candy from his mother only slightly disobeys the seventh commandment, which forbids stealing, and consequently he deserves only a light punishment.

By contrast, consider Cain, who appears in the illustration. So wicked was he that, out of envy, he killed his good brother, Abel. Cain disobeyed the fifth commandment seriously; he committed a horrible sin. Thus the Lord punished him even in this life, condemning him to wander over the earth without ever having peace. And in the next life?

Whoever grievously disobeys God's commandments deserves hell.

**"God's commandments are light to the loving, heavy to the fearful."**

St. Thomas Aquinas

***What is sin?***

**Sin is an offense given to God by disobeying His law.**

***How many kinds of sin are there?***

**There are two kinds of sin: original sin and actual sin.**

***What is original sin?***

**Original sin is the sin which mankind committed in Adam, the head of the human race, and which every descendant of Adam inherits by bodily generation.**

*Original Sin* Benvenuti-Alinari

Here we find depicted the temptation and sin of Adam and Eve.

They were our first parents, created by God and placed by Him in the terrestrial paradise, where they lived in complete happiness, until the envious devil disguised himself as a serpent and tempted them. To test their fidelity God had forbidden Adam and Eve to eat the fruit of a certain tree. But the devil urged, "Eat of this fruit; you will become like God!" Eve, letting herself be persuaded, picked the fruit, ate of it, and gave some to Adam. Thus, with the hope of becoming as great as God, they disobeyed His command and committed a grievous sin.

In punishment for their sin, Adam and Eve lost sanctifying grace and the right to heaven. They became subject to suffering and death, and to a strong inclination to evil. Moreover, God sent them out of the earthly paradise.

On account of the sin of Adam, we, his descendants, come into this world with original sin, that is, deprived of sanctifying grace. However, God did not abandon man after Adam fell into sin, but He sent into the world His Son, our Lord Jesus Christ, to free man from his sins and to reopen to him the gates of heaven. Our Savior instituted the Sacrament of Baptism to take away original sin.

**"For just as by the disobedience of the one man the many were constituted sinners, so also by the obedience of the one the many will be constituted just."** Rom. 5:19

*The Immaculate Conception* Reni-Alinari

***Was any human person ever preserved from original sin?***

**The Blessed Virgin Mary was preserved from original sin in view of the merits of her divine Son; and this privilege is called her Immaculate Conception.**

You are all fair, all pure, O Mary, and there is in you no stain of original sin!

Mary would have incurred original sin in the usual way from her parents, had she not been preserved in view of the merits of her divine Son.

But because God had from all eternity destined Mary to be the Mother of His Son, He kept her immune from every stain of sin from the first moment of her existence.

The soul of the Blessed Virgin was created as pure and spotless as Eve's soul, but whereas Eve stained her soul with sin, our Lady kept herself immaculate to the end of her life.

The Immaculate Virgin and the devil are two extremes that never meet.

The Immaculate Virgin is our heavenly Mother. Let us pray to her so that sin may cease upon the earth: **"That sin may have an end, and iniquity may be abolished"** (Dn. 9:24).

Let us love our Lady with filial hearts and ask her to preserve our souls pure and immaculate.

**You are the glory of Jerusalem, you are the joy of Israel, you are the honor of our people, O Mary!**

*The Betrayal of Judas* Prell-Ed. Haufstaengl-Monaco

***What is actual sin?***

**Actual sin is any willful thought, desire, word, action or omission forbidden by the law of God.**

Original sin is not the only kind of sin; there is another kind, called actual sin, and this is the sin we ourselves commit.

In the above illustration, we see Judas in a most turbulent state of mind, because he is about to enter into conspiracy with the enemies of Jesus; he is about to betray our Lord, to sell Him for thirty pieces of silver.

His betrayal was an actual sin because he himself committed it knowingly and voluntarily.

Actual sin is an offense against the law of God committed with knowledge and consent of the will by anyone who has the use of reason.

Young children and the insane cannot commit sin, because they do not have the use of reason. Nor can a person sin who is not conscious of doing evil, for he does not have the will to offend our Lord.

However, a person who, knowing he is offending God, yet retains an evil thought, says bad words, does bad deeds, or fails to do his duty, commits an actual sin.

**"The cause of sin is the will's not holding to the rule of reason and divine law."** St. Thomas Aquinas

The Lord says, **"Flee from sins as from the face of a serpent, for if you come near them, they will take hold of you."** Eccl. 21:2

*Ambush* G. D. Quadrone-Borgi

***How many kinds of actual sin are there?***

**There are two kinds of actual sin: mortal sin and venial sin.**

***What is a mortal sin?***

**Mortal sin is a grievous offense against the law of God.**

When one has committed a sin, he can tell, by means of his conscience, whether that sin was mortal or venial. He does this by asking himself if 1) the thought, desire, word, action, or omission was seriously wrong or considered seriously wrong; 2) if he was mindful of the serious wrong; 3) if he fully consented to it. If his conscience tells him that all these three conditions were present, then he committed a mortal sin. If even only one of those conditions was not present, then his sin was venial, not mortal.

The fierce-looking men in the illustration are waiting with drawn swords for their intended victim, who is about to enter. They know what they are doing; they have decided to kill the man and are thus acting with full consent of the will. Since murder is strictly forbidden by the law of God, they commit a mortal sin.

Whoever commits a mortal sin loses God's friendship, His grace, and all the merits acquired. He ceases to earn new merits and deserves hell.

However, one in the state of mortal sin should perform good actions, not only to keep from becoming worse, but also to dispose himself to regain the grace of God by a good confession or an act of perfect contrition with the intention of going to confession.

**"God is faithful and will not permit you to be tempted beyond your strength."**

1 Cor. 10:13

*The True Cryptogram* Cei-Brogi

***What is a venial sin?***

**Venial sin is a less serious offense against the law of God, which does not deprive the soul of sanctifying grace, and which can be pardoned even without sacramental confession.**

What rascals! Not a day passes in which they do not fail to do some mischief! Here they are, stealing grapes from someone's garden.

These youngsters should not take the grapes, which do not belong to them, because in the seventh commandment our Lord has forbidden the taking of other people's belongings. In stealing the grapes, the boys disobey God; consequently, they commit sin.

A mortal sin? No, for they are taking only a few grapes, and are doing only slight injury to the owner. Possibly some of them have never received religious instruction and do not know that they are doing wrong. In conclusion, they are committing, at most, a **venial sin.**

Thus a sin is venial when the evil done is not seriously wrong or when the evil done is seriously wrong but the sinner sincerely believes it is only slightly wrong, or does not give full consent to it. Venial sin does not take away God's grace, but it diminishes our fervor, weakens our power to resist mortal sin, and merits God's punishment in this life or in purgatory.

The Lord says, **"He that contemns small things, shall fall little by little."**

Eccl. 19:1

*Noah's Sacrifice* Benvenuti-Alinari

***What is the first commandment of God?***

**The first commandment of God is: I am the Lord thy God; thou shalt not have strange gods before me.**

***What are we commanded by the first commandment?***

**By the first commandment we are commanded to offer to God alone the supreme worship that is due Him.**

Only Noah and those in the ark with him were saved from the deluge. After he left the ark, Noah built an altar, and offered the Lord sacrifices to adore and thank Him.

Pleased with Noah's sacrifice, God blessed him and his family. He assured him that He would never again send a deluge, and He sealed His promise by causing a rainbow to shine in the heavens.

Sacrifices are offered only to God as the Creator and Lord of the universe.

In giving us His law, God announces Himself as the supreme authority: "I am the Lord thy God!"

First of all, He commands us not to believe, love, adore, or serve anyone or anything but Him.

We **believe** in God by knowing Him and accepting His teachings. We **love** Him by observing His commandments. We **adore** Him by recognizing Him as our supreme Master and acknowledging our complete dependence upon Him. We **serve** Him through prayer and a Christian life.

We owe God exterior as well as interior worship, because our bodies, as well as our souls, belong to Him.

**"Surely to obey in simple tranquillity and unsolicitous confidence is the noblest conceivable worship man can pay to his Creator."** Cardinal Newman

*Belshazzar's Feast* PretiMattia-Anderson

***What does the first commandment forbid?***

**The first commandment forbids impiety, superstition, simony, sacrilege, apostasy, heresy, and indifferentism.**

***When does a person sin by impiety?***

**A person sins by impiety when he refuses God every form of worship.**

In commanding us to give God the honor due Him, the first commandment forbids impiety.

Impiety is the refusal to offer God the supreme worship that is His due. The impious person is he who never goes to church, does not perform his Easter duty, and ridicules God, the commandments, the saints and holy things.

The Holy Spirit tells us, **"To God the wicked and his wickedness are hateful alike"** (Wis. 14:9). And the Lord punishes the loathsome sin of impiety with dreadful chastisements.

In the illustration, we see Belshazzar, an impious king who did not fear the Lord. In mockery of God and religion, he once ordered that his banquet guests be served with sacred and very precious vessels stolen from the temple of the Lord in Jerusalem. But at once a hand appeared writing mysterious words on the wall of the palace. Terrified, the king summoned Daniel the prophet to interpret the writing. It was the Lord's condemnation of him. The words on the wall were **Mane, Thecel, Phares,** and they meant: God has numbered your kingdom and has finished it. You have been weighed in the balance and found wanting. Your kingdom has been divided and will be given to others.

Indeed, on that very night, Belshazzar's enemies killed him.

**"The hope of the wicked is as dust, which is blown away with the wind, and as thin froth which is dispersed by the storm."** Wis. 5:15

*Moses Breaking the Tablets of Laws* Schnorr

***When does a person sin by superstition?***

**A person sins by superstition when he attributes to a creature a power that belongs to God alone, as when he makes use of charms or spells, believes in dreams or fortune-telling, or goes to spiritists.**

In the illustration, we see Moses about to smash the tablets of the law. He had ascended Mount Sinai to receive the commandments from God, and had remained there forty days in conversation with Him. The Hebrews, living in tents in the desert, had grown tired of waiting for him and had said to one another, "Moses will not return; something must have happened to him. Let us make gods that may go before us." They therefore had made a golden calf and offered sacrifices to it, as if to the true God. When Moses came down from the mount and saw them adoring an idol, he angrily broke the tablets. Then, after destroying the calf, he punished those who had committed the grievous sin.

Superstition is any practice which gives false worship to God or undue honor to creatures. It includes everything from idolatry to such nonsensical practices as: the use of charms and spells, belief in dreams, fortune-telling, spiritism, astrological horoscopes, unlucky days and numbers, omens, as for example, breaking a mirror, walking under a ladder, having our path crossed by a black cat, and so on.

Superstitious practices are a violation of the first commandment of God, because they attribute to created things powers that God reserves to Himself.

"Superstition recurs in all ages," wrote G. K. Chesterton, "and especially in rationalistic ages." The serious and intelligent are not superstitious.

**"You shall fear the Lord your God, and shall serve him only."**

Dt. 6:13

*St. Peter Disputes with Simon Magus* Tiarini-Alinari

***When does a person sin by simony?***

**A person sins by simony when he buys or sells sacred or scriptural things or positions.**

***When does a person sin by sacrilege?***

**A person sins by sacrilege when he mistreats sacred persons, places, or things.**

The term **simony** comes from Simon Magus, a very clever man who deceived the people of Samaria by the practice of magic. Through St. Philip's preaching, he, too, became a Christian. Then, when St. Peter and St. John came from Jerusalem so that by the laying on of their hands the faithful might receive the Holy Spirit, Simon Magus attempted to buy from them the power of giving the Holy Spirit. "Your money go to destruction with you," retorted St. Peter sternly.

**Simony is a sin because it depreciates spiritual things, lowering them to the level of the material.**

**It is simony, for example, to sell rosaries, medals or other religious articles for more than their ordinary price on account of a blessing they have.**

**Sacrilege** is the irreverent treatment of sacred persons, places, or things. It is a sacrilege to mistreat a person consecrated to God, to receive the sacraments unworthily, to commit acts of impurity or of violence in a church or consecrated cemetery, to steal sacred objects, etc.

The Lord says, **"Son, keep my commandments, and you shall live. And my law as the apple of your eye."** Prv. 7:2

*The Iconoclasts* Domenico Morelli-Alinari

***When does a person sin by heresy?***

**A person sins by heresy when, although a baptized Catholic, he refuses to accept one or more of the truths revealed by God and taught by the Catholic Church.**

One example of heresy was iconoclasm. The iconoclasts held that veneration of holy images is unlawful. As shown in the illustration, they entered churches to break, burn and trample upon statues and pictures, injuring those who exposed the images for the veneration of the faithful.

Holy Mother Church teaches that it is right to show respect to the statues and pictures of Christ, the Blessed Virgin and of the saints because of whom they represent, just as it is right to show respect to the statues of national heroes and to the pictures of loved ones.

We do not pray to statues and pictures, but to Christ and the saints, whom they represent. When we contemplate images of our Lord, the Blessed Virgin and the saints, our thoughts fly to them and we feel a desire to pray to them and to imitate them.

We honor the saints in heaven because they practiced great virtue when they were on earth, and because in honoring those who are the chosen friends of God, we honor God Himself.

We ask the saints to offer their prayers to God for us because they are with Him and have great love for us.

**"To the saints honor must be paid as friends of Christ, as sons and heirs of God."**

St. John of Damascus

***When does a person sin by indifferentism?***

**A person sins by indifferentism when he holds that one religion is as good as another and that all religions are equally true and pleasing to God, or that one is free to accept or reject any or all religions.**

*St. Stephen Before the Judges* Yuanes-Anderson

St. Stephen, one of the seven deacons elected by the Apostles, was the first Christian to seal his faith with martyrdom. Filled with the Holy Spirit and with fortitude, he preached to everyone that Jesus is truly the promised Messiah. No one could withstand the wisdom of his words.

The illustration depicts him speaking to the members of the Sanhedrin, who had gathered to judge him for his faith. Stephen spoke with such ardor that his face seemed the face of an angel. The doctors of the Law, unable to reply to him, gnashed their teeth in rage and blocked their ears so as not to hear him.

Even in our own day, there are people who deliberately reject belief in God and Christ, just as there are those who lead bad lives and who, to justify their wickedness, try to convince themselves that there is no God, no religion.

Others, although convinced of the fact that the Catholic Church is the true Church of Jesus Christ, the Son of God, hesitate to accept the Catholic Faith because of the sacrifices that are connected with it, such as a stricter moral code, confession and the marriage laws. Consequently, they may be heard to say that "one religion is as good as another," but no one can seriously believe this, because there can be only one true religion, and false religions certainly cannot be as good as the true one.

We must take care to safeguard our faith by studying our religion well, by living a good life, by good reading and by refraining from association with enemies of the Church.

**"Ignorance of religion is the cause of the innumerable evils which afflict society in our day."**

Pope Benedict XV

*The Punished Blasphemer* Dorè-Garzanti

***What are we commanded by the second commandment of God, "Thou shalt not take the name of the Lord thy God in vain"?***

**By the second commandment, we are commanded always...to speak with reverence of God, of the saints, and of holy things.**

God's name is most holy, and it is to be pronounced with holy respect and reverence. St. Jerome said that there is no sin more serious than blasphemy, which is insulting language expressing contempt for God, either directly or through His saints and holy things. The law of Moses, in fact, ordered that anyone caught blaspheming should be driven out of the city and stoned to death.

"At the name of Jesus, every knee should bend," says St. Paul. Therefore, God's name must never be used in vain, that is, to express surprise, anger or impatience, to jest, or out of habit, without thought of paying God honor. The same must be said for the names of the Blessed Virgin and the saints.

By honoring a name, we honor the one related to it. We show love and reverence to God's name by using it reverently in prayer, by bowing our heads at the name of Jesus, and by speaking reverently of the Blessed Virgin, the angels, the saints, the Church, and persons, places, or things dedicated to God's service.

**"May the name of the Lord be blessed both now and forever."**

Ps. 113:2

*St. Peter's Denial* M. Len Nain-Alinari

***What are we commanded by the second commandment of God, "Thou shalt not take the name of the Lord thy God in vain"?***

**By the second commandment, we are commanded always...to be truthful in taking oaths and faithful to them....**

**"Let your speech,"** said our Lord, **"be 'Yes, yes'; 'no, no'!"** (Mt. 6:27)

By those words, Jesus meant that we should be simple in our speech, and not take needless oaths.

Anyone who swears, calls upon God to witness to the truth of what he says. An oath is a very serious thing which must be taken for very good reasons, that is, when it is useful in having our word accepted in matters which concern the glory of God or the good of our neighbor or of ourselves.

The second commandment forbids us to swear falsely, that is, to confirm by oath what one knows is not true.

Even St. Peter once took a false oath. When Jesus was imprisoned, St. Peter followed Him from afar. However, a little servant recognized him. "You too," she said, "are one of the disciples of Jesus!" In fear, Peter swore three times that he did not know Jesus. Then the cock crowed, and Peter remembered Jesus' prediction of the sin he had just committed. Leaving the courtyard, he went out and wept bitterly.

The second commandment also forbids us to swear to do what is wrong. If one takes an oath to do what is wrong, useless, or impossible, he is not obliged to keep it.

**"My brethren,"** says the Apostle St. James, **"do not swear; either by heaven or by the earth, or any other oath."** Jas. 5:12

*Anna's Vow* From The Quiver

***What are we commanded by the second commandment of God, "Thou shalt not take the name of the Lord thy God in vain"?***

**By the second commandment, we are commanded always...to be faithful to our vows.**

The lovely woman in the illustration is Anna, of whom we read in the holy Bible. She was childless until she made a vow to the Lord that if He would grant her the gift of motherhood, she would consecrate her firstborn to Him. God heard her, and that good mother, faithful to her vow, took her son Samuel to the High Priest to be brought up in the temple, in the love and service of God.

A vow is a deliberate promise made to God by which a person binds himself under pain of sin to do something that is especially pleasing to God.

The most important vows are the public vows of poverty, chastity, and obedience taken by members of religious orders and congregations.

A vow should always be made after due reflection and the advice of a prudent spiritual director.

If we vow to do a good deed, we must do it; if we make a vow or promise to God, we must keep it.

He who fails to keep the word he has given to another, acts wrongly and may be called a man without honor. Similarly, he who fails to fulfill promises and vows made to our Lord, offends Him, and sins.

**"If you have vowed anything to God, defer not to pay it."** Eccl. 5:3

***What are we commanded by the third commandment, "Remember thou keep holy the Lord's day"?***

**By the third commandment we are commanded to worship God in a special manner on Sunday, the Lord's day.**

*Magistrate Cicogna Assists at Mass* — Palmo il giov.-Alinari

God left us six days of the week for ourselves, but He reserved one day entirely for Himself, that we might sanctify it by offering Him special acts of worship. Sunday is the Lord's day. Besides Sundays, there are other feastdays during the year.

Days reserved for the Lord are most advantageous to the individual and to society. They benefit the individual by giving him the opportunity to pay more attention to God and by allowing him to enjoy needed rest. They benefit society by lifting men to a higher level and uniting them in a common bond of brotherhood.

Observe the picture. Ordinary women are shown at holy Mass kneeling beside the Venetian Magistrate Cicogna. Around the altar, every trace of social inequality has disappeared; the rich and the poor are on the same level, offering the same Sacrifice and nourishing themselves with the same celestial Bread.

The Venetian Magistrate, as the supreme authority of the state, offers a shining example of fidelity to religious duties. At the right of the picture we see a woman who has entered to beg him for a hearing. He is replying that she will have to wait, for he must perform his religious duty before his official duty.

The Church commands us to worship God on Sundays and all holy days of obligation by assisting at the holy Sacrifice of the Mass.

The Sacrifice of the Mass offers us an opportunity to gain great spiritual benefits, and the more devoutly we participate at Mass, the more graces we obtain.

Sunday is also an appropriate day for performing some good deeds, for reading good Catholic literature, and for enjoying Catholic radio and TV.

**"To me nothing is so consoling or so thrilling as the Mass, the greatest action that can take place on earth."** Cardinal Newman

*Alabaster Workshop* Alinari

***What is forbidden by the third commandment of God, "Remember thou keep holy the Lord's day"?***

**By the third commandment of God all unnecessary servile work on Sunday is forbidden.**

The holy Bible narrates that when the Lord created the universe, He worked for six days and rested on the seventh: **"God blessed the seventh day and sanctified it, because on it he had rested from all his work"** (Gn. 2:3). God did so, as a way of telling us that we must rest on Sundays. In the third commandment, therefore, He forbids servile work on that day.

Servile work, illustrated in the scene above, is that which requires labor of body rather than of mind, such as farming, mechanical and industrial labor, even though one does them for pleasure and without any gain.

Reading, writing, typewriting, studying, drawing, playing music, traveling, hunting, fishing, and the like are not servile works.

Servile work may be allowed on Sunday when the honor of God, our own need, or that of our neighbor requires it. In doubt, one should consult his pastor before beginning the work.

The Church does not forbid lawful amusements on Sunday, as long as they do not interfere with the Sunday obligations.

**"Six days shall you do work: on the seventh day is the sabbath, the rest holy to the Lord."** Ex. 31:15

*Joseph's Meeting with His Father* Schnorr

***What are we commanded by the fourth commandment of God, "Honor thy father and thy mother"?***

**By the fourth commandment we are commanded to respect and love our parents, to obey them in all that is not sinful, and to help them when they are in need.**

Joseph, son of Jacob, was sold into slavery in Egypt by his brothers, but the Lord aided him and he eventually became Viceroy of Egypt. He saved the Egyptians from starvation in time of famine, and when he learned that his father and brothers were suffering hunger, he sent for them and settled them in the most fertile region of the country. How he loved and honored his father!

One **respects** his parents when he speaks and acts towards them with proper deference, accepts their corrections readily, seeks their advice in important decisions, and bears with charity their faults. One **loves** his parents when he tries to please and help them. Children should **obey** the lawful commands of their parents as long as they live under their authority, because parents hold God's place in the home. However, one must obey God rather than parents or others in authority when their commands are against the law of God. Lastly, children must **aid** their parents when they are in need.

On their part, parents have the obligation of caring for their children, giving them proper religious training, and providing for their bodily welfare.

**"Honor thy father and thy mother, that thou mayest be long-lived upon the land which the Lord thy God will give thee."** Ex. 20:12

*The Death of Absalom* Schnorr

***What does the fourth commandment of God, "Honor thy father and thy mother," forbid?***

**The fourth commandment forbids disrespect, unkindness, and disobedience to parents and lawful superiors.**

How painful it is to see someone offend or even insult his parents, to whom, after God, he is indebted for his very life!

Pictured here is Absalom, the handsome son of the holy King David. Although his father's favorite, the ungrateful young man rebelled against the king, assembled an army and attempted to seize David's throne and kingdom. But God punished Absalom. His army was routed, and he himself, fleeing from David's soldiers, was overtaken and killed when his hair got caught in the branches of a tree.

Children show **disrespect** and **unkindness** to their parents by talking back to them, refusing their correction, causing them great sorrow, etc.

Children are guilty of **disobedience** when they refuse to do what their parents command, as, for example, to avoid bad companions, sinful reading or immoral amusements, to receive the sacraments and religious instruction, and so forth.

No matter how high children rise in the world, they always owe their parents honor and respect, for they are God's representatives even if they have remained in humble conditions. In all the splendor of his majesty, King Solomon descended from his throne to meet his mother and pay her honor.

The fourth commandment also forbids disrespect, unkindness and disobedience to lawful superiors.

**"Blessed are the obedient, for God will never suffer them to go astray."**

St. Francis de Sales

*David Insulted* Schnorr

***What are we commanded by the fifth commandment of God, "Thou shalt not kill"?***

**By the fifth commandment we are commanded to take proper care of our own spiritual and bodily well-being and that of our neighbor.**

While King David was in flight from Jerusalem, a man named Semei, for whom King David had done many favors, came to curse him and throw stones at him. David's soldiers wanted to kill him, but the King would not permit it. "Let him alone," he said. "It is the Lord permitting it." Such gentleness disarmed Semei, who repented and became a faithful follower of his king.

**"A new commandment I give you,"** said Jesus to His disciples, **"that you love one another: that as I have loved you, you also love one another"** (Jn. 13:34). This is what the fifth commandment orders.

We must love everyone. We are all brothers, because we are all children of God. We must love both the good and the bad, and even those who do us injury. We must forgive them.

Whenever we are able, we must also help those who are in need. Jesus said, **"Amen I say to you, as long as you did not do it for one of these least ones, you did not do it for me"** (Mt. 25:45).

Just as we are obliged to use prudent means in order to preserve our health, we are also obliged to have prudent regard for the health of those under our care.

If we have injured anyone spiritually or physically, we must beg pardon and make amends.

The Apostle of love says, **"And this commandment we have from God, that he who loves God, should love his brother also."** 1 Jn. 4:21

*Abel's Murder* Salv. Rosa-Alinari

***What does the fifth commandment of God, "Thou shalt not kill," forbid?***

**The fifth commandment forbids murder....**

The tragic story of Cain and Abel powerfully illustrates violation of God's fifth commandment. Cain was passionately jealous of his brother Abel, whose prayers and sacrifices, unlike his own, were pleasing to the Lord.

One day Cain asked Abel to go for a walk with him, and when they were in the fields, he leaped upon his younger brother and killed him. Bitter remorse at once began to torment him. God condemned Cain to be a wanderer on the earth, and He punished him for having shed his brother's blood.

Murder is the unjust killing of a human being.

Murder is a great sin, because it is an infringement on the right of God's dominion over human life. God created us; He alone has supreme dominion over our life.

The life of another may be taken in order to protect one's own life or that of a neighbor, provided no other means of protection is effective.

Another's life may not be taken to end his sufferings. Thus, euthanasia, or "mercy killing," is murder.

Likewise, an unborn child may never be directly killed, even to save the life of the mother, for that child has the same right to life as any other person.

**"We must be kind and loving, merciful and just to all, and recognize in every human being, whatever his race or color, the God who made him and the inalienable rights with which He endowed him."**

Richard J. Cardinal Cushing, D.D.

***What does the fifth commandment of God, "Thou shalt not kill," forbid?***

**The fifth commandment forbids...suicide....**

*The Suicide of Judas* Schnorr

This man with the convulsed features and wild, unkempt hair is the traitor, Judas. After betraying our Lord, he was torn by remorse and wandered about in the woods in desperation until finally, he hanged himself from a tree. Thus, to the sin of betrayal, Judas added the sin of suicide.

Suicide is self-murder, and it is a great sin.

Our life belongs to God, not to us. We cannot end it when we wish.

He is not courageous who commits suicide; true courage consists in taking life as it comes, with resignation and love of God, never forgetting that "the sole purpose of life in time is to gain merit for life in eternity" (St. Augustine).

Holy Mother Church denies Christian burial to those who knowingly and voluntarily commit suicide. Many who commit suicide are not responsible.

We are obliged to take reasonable care of our health and to do nothing which could injure or destroy it.

It is a sin to risk one's life without a sufficiently good reason.

It is, however, lawful and very meritorious to risk one's life in order to gain eternal life, as do martyrs, or in order to save others from spiritual death, as do missionaries, or from physical death, as do doctors, nurses, rescue workers and others.

**"Suicide is the ultimate and absolute evil, the refusal to take an interest in existence; the refusal to take the oath of loyalty to life."**

G. K. Chesterton

*The Attack at the New Inn* Goja-Anderson

***What does the fifth commandment of God, "Thou shalt not kill," forbid?***

**The fifth commandment forbids...fighting, anger, hatred, revenge, drunkenness, and bad example.**

With these words: "Blessed are the peacemakers, for they shall be called sons of God," Jesus willed to teach us that true children of God are always at peace with everyone.

The fifth commandment forbids: **fighting,** which is violent physical combat; **anger,** which is a strong emotion of displeasure and a desire to punish the offender; **hatred,** which is strong aversion or detestation coupled with ill will towards anyone; **revenge,** which is the desire to punish someone excessively, from a motive of anger; **drunkenness,** which is excessive use of alcoholic drink to the extent of losing one's reason; and **scandal,** which is giving another, by any evil word or deed, the occasion to sin.

Scandal is a very great evil, and God will ask an account of the evil occasioned by wicked encouragement and bad example. **"Woe to the man through whom scandal comes"** (Mt. 18:7).

**"You shall love your neighbor as yourself."** Mt. 22:39

**"Forgive whatever you have against anyone, that your father in heaven may also forgive you your offenses. But if you do not forgive, neither will your father in heaven forgive you your offenses."** Mk. 11:25-26

***What are we commanded by the sixth commandment of God, "Thou shalt not commit adultery"?***

**By the sixth commandment we are commanded to be pure and modest in our behavior.**

*Innocence*

Kaspar Schlebiner-Ed.
Die Christliche Kunst

"The virtue of chastity," explained Pius XII, "does not mean that we are insensible to the urge of concupiscence, but that we subordinate it to reason and the law of grace, by striving wholeheartedly after what is noblest in human and Christian life."

We must respect our body because it is God's masterpiece, the work of His hands, and because God dwells in us with His presence and His grace. For this reason, St. Paul exhorts us: **"Glorify God and bear him in your body"** (1 Cor. 6:20). And he admonishes us: **"Do you not know that your members are the temple of the Holy Spirit?"** (1 Cor. 6:19)

An artist takes jealous care of his masterpiece. Similarly, God has jealous regard for His masterpiece and does not want to see it degraded and soiled, reduced to an instrument of indecent pleasures. Churches and sacred vessels deserve our respect, but our body is much more sacred than buildings of stone or vessels of metal. **"If anyone destroys the temple of God, him will God destroy; for holy is the temple of God, and this temple you are"** (1 Cor. 3:17).

**"The impure cannot love God; and those who are without love of God cannot really be pure. Purity prepares the soul for love, and love confirms the soul in purity."**

Cardinal Newman

*The Deluge* Dorè-Garzanti

***What does the sixth commandment of God, "Thou shalt not commit adultery," forbid?***

**The sixth commandment forbids all impurity and immodesty in words, looks, and actions, whether alone or with others.**

At the time of the Patriarch Noah, the enormity of men's sins, especially the sins of impurity, provoked divine Justice to decree a terrible punishment: the deluge. The floodgates of the heavens were opened and it rained incessantly for forty days and forty nights. The water reached the mountain tops, submerging all living creatures in its depths. Only Noah, whom God loved for his goodness, his family, and the animals with him in the Ark escaped drowning.

The sixth commandment forbids **immoral actions** with oneself or another, **unchaste words,** and evil-intentioned **looks** at things, persons or pictures which can arouse the sexual appetite.

God buried the inhabitants of Sodom and Gomorrah under a downpour of fire, because of their unmentionable vices. The gravity of the punishment indicates the gravity of this sin.

Let us heed the warning of the Apostle: **"Immorality and every uncleanness or covetousness let it not even be named among you, as becomes saints; or obscenity or foolish talk or scurrility, which are out of place; but rather thanksgiving. For know this and understand, that no fornicator, or unclean person, or covetous one (for that is idolatry) has any inheritance in the kingdom of Christ and God"** (Eph. 5:3-6).

**"This is the will of God, your sanctification; that you abstain from immorality; that everyone of you learn how to possess his vessel in holiness and honor, not in the passion of lust like the Gentiles who do not know God."**

1 Thess. 4:3-5

***What are the chief dangers to the virtue of chastity?***

**The chief dangers to the virtue of chastity are: idleness, sinful curiosity, bad companions, drinking, immodest dress, and indecent books, plays, motion pictures, television programs and videocassettes.**

*St. Paul's Preaching at Ephesus* — Eustache le Seur-Alinari

In the illustration, St. Paul is pictured with the Christians of Ephesus, who are bringing to him all their evil books to be burned in a great bonfire in the public square.

Indecent books which describe sinful love and relations, newspapers and magazines filled with lewd pictures, and obscene programs, films and plays are dangers to the virtue of chastity. Other dangers are idleness, which is the father of sin; sinful curiosity, which desires to know everything, see everything, and try everything; companions, whose behavior is unchaste; excess in drinking, which arouses passions; and immodesty in dress.

To preserve the virtue of chastity, we must avoid all these occasions of sin, seek God's help through prayer when tempted, go to confession and Holy Communion often, have a special devotion to the Blessed Virgin, remember that God sees us at all times, and finally, practice mortification, particularly of the eyes, of the palate, and of the imagination.

**"Watch and pray, that you may not enter into temptation. The spirit indeed is willing, but the flesh is weak."** Mk. 14:38

**"Be sober, be watchful! For your adversary the devil, as a roaring lion, goes about seeking someone to devour. Resist him, steadfast in the faith, knowing that the same suffering befalls your brethren all over the world."** 1 Pt. 5:8-9

*The Owner of the Vineyard* Conti

***What are we commanded by the seventh commandment of God, "Thou shalt not steal"?***

**By the seventh commandment we are commanded to respect what belongs to others, to live up to our business agreements and to pay our just debts.**

The seventh commandment orders us to be honest in everything we do, and to pay our debts. We must never incur debts beyond our means to pay, but once we have contracted a debt, we are under moral obligation to pay.

The seventh commandment also obliges employers to pay their workers a just wage, one proportionate to the type and amount of work accomplished.

One day Jesus told the beautiful parable of the vineyard keeper. A householder went out one morning, gathered a good number of workmen, designated their daily wage and sent them to work in his vineyard. Perhaps it was a day of harvest, and since there were not enough workingmen, he also sent to work additional men whom he met later on in the day. At nightfall, the owner handed all the workers the wages they had agreed upon. But those who had come earlier complained that they were treated the same as those who had come later. The owner replied to one of them, "Friend, I do you no injustice; did you not agree with me for a denarius? Take what is yours and go; I choose to give to this last even as to you" (Mt. 20:13-15).

Thus the seventh commandment imposes on us the virtue of justice: giving to each his due.

**"You shall not refuse the hire of the needy, and the poor,"** the Lord says, **"but you shall pay him the price of his labor the same day, before the going down of the sun, because he is poor, and with it maintains his life, lest he cry against you to the Lord, and it be reputed to you for a sin."**

Dt. 24:14-16

***What does the seventh commandment, "Thou shalt not steal," forbid?***

**Besides stealing, the seventh commandment forbids cheating, unjust keeping of what belongs to others, unjust damage to the property of others, and the accepting of bribes by public officials.**

*Heliodorus Driven from the Temple* Dorè-Garzanti

We have the right to our own possessions. Whoever takes possession of another person's property, either secretly or openly and violently, transgresses God's seventh commandment and is a thief.

The Lord condemns to hell those who seriously violate this commandment and die without making reparation. Often, He punishes them with grave penalties even in this life.

We find an example of God's punishment in the biblical story of Heliodorus, minister of the king of Syria, who was sent by his wicked sovereign to steal the treasures and offerings of the temple of Jerusalem. No sooner had he crossed the threshold when celestial warriors appeared, threw him to the ground, and whipped him soundly.

Besides theft and robbery, the seventh commandment forbids taking advantage of another's ignorance or need, as, for instance, by overcharging, using false weights, misrepresenting the value of goods sold, charging excessive interest, etc. It is sinful to willfully damage another's property. **Employers** sin by denying laborers a just, living wage. **Employees** sin by wasting time, working carelessly, or neglecting to take reasonable care of their employers' property. **Public officials** sin by accepting bribes.

Petty violations of the seventh commandment must be strictly avoided and punished, or they will lead to serious sins.

**"Better is a little with justice, than great revenues with iniquity."**

Prv. 16:8

*Cyrus Returns the Vases to the Temple* Dorè-Garzanti

***Are we obliged to repair damage unjustly done to the property of others?***

**We are obliged to repair damage unjustly done to the property of others, or to pay the amount of damage, as far as we are able.**

***Are we obliged to restore to the owner stolen goods, or their value?***

**We are obliged to restore to the owner stolen goods, or their value, whenever we are able.**

The picture illustrates a beautiful example of restitution in the holy Bible. The Israelites had been defeated by King Nebuchadnezzar and carried off to slavery in Babylon. Later, King Cyrus of Persia conquered Babylon. He had scarcely ascended the throne, when he granted them permission to return to their native land and to rebuild the Temple. At that time he restored to them the sacred vases and precious objects which had been stolen.

One who has stolen must make restitution. He who could do so and does not will not obtain pardon, even if he declares himself repentant. St. Augustine writes: "If the stolen goods can be restored and the thief does not make restitution, even sacramental confession will do him no good."

A person who deliberately assists another in stealing, even though he receives none of the loot, may be bound to make restitution if the other person does not do so.

Restitution, however, may be made secretly, without letting the owner know that it is being made.

If the owner is dead, restitution must be made to his heirs. If there are no heirs, the goods or their value must be given to the poor or pious causes.

**"If any man hurt a field or a vineyard, and put in his beast to feed upon that which is other men's: he shall restore the best of whatsoever he has in his own field, or in his vineyard, according to the estimation of the damage."** Ex. 22:5

**"The beginning of a good way is to do justice; and this is more acceptable with God, than to offer sacrifices."** Prv. 16:5

*Behold, the Man!* Ciseri-Alinari

***What are we commanded by the eighth commandment of God, "Thou shalt not bear false witness against thy neighbor"?***

**By the eighth commandment we are commanded to speak the truth in all things.**

When our Lord was brought before the high priest Caiaphas, He was confronted with false testimonies, insults, groundless accusations, and the complete absence of legality. But the Divine Master remained sublimely tranquil, serene and majestic. "I adjure you by the living God," cried the high priest, "that you tell us whether you are the Christ, the Son of God!"

Jesus knew that such a declaration would cost Him His life. Nevertheless, to teach us that truth must be professed with courage, when legitimately questioned, He answered, "You have said it." And then came the sentence: "He is liable to death!"

Christ's enemies next led Him to Pilate and accused Him of having rebelled against Roman authority by making Himself a king. Pilate questioned Jesus, "Are you the king of the Jews?" Jesus answered, "My kingdom is not of this world." "You are then a king?" insisted Pilate with surprise. "You say it," affirmed Jesus. "I am a king. This is why I was born, and why I have come into the world, to bear witness to the truth."

"I am the truth," Jesus said, and He taught us by His example to speak the truth frankly, when it is necessary, even at the cost of our life.

If we are justly questioned by one who has the right to know the truth, we must say the truth. However, if we are questioned by persons who have no right to know the truth, we can give an evasive answer.

**"Everyone who is of the truth, hears my voice."** Jn. 18:37

*Simplicity* — Veronese-Alinari

***What are we commanded by the eighth commandment?***

**By the eighth commandment we are commanded to speak the truth in all things, but especially in what concerns the good name and honor of others.**

A good name is a most precious possession. The eighth commandment obliges us to respect the good name of our neighbor by not making known his faults when we have no right to do so and by not making false accusations against him.

It is our duty to think well and to speak well of others.

Only God can penetrate to the interior of man's conscience and scrutinize his intentions. Thus He alone can judge with truth and justice. "There is one lawgiver and judge," says St. James, "he who is able to destroy and to save. But you who judge your neighbor, who are you?"

Observe the symbolic representation of simplicity by Paul Veronese. The lady is seated unaffectedly, without pomp. Her gaze is serene, frank and sincere. She is holding up a small ermine, a little animal famous for the whiteness of its fur and its innate horror of filth. This meaningful illustration reminds us that the disciple of Christ should be simple and sincere, and have a genuine horror of all uncharitable talk. St. Paul teaches, "Charity is kind, thinks no evil, does not rejoice over wickedness, but rejoices with the truth...bears with all things, believes all things, endures all things" (1 Cor. 13:4-7).

**"A good name is better than great riches."** Prv. 22:1

*Joseph's Brothers Showing His Clothes to His Father* Velasquez-Anderson

***What does the eighth commandment of God, "Thou shalt not bear false witness against thy neighbor," forbid?***

**The eighth commandment forbids lies....**

In the Holy Bible we read that after Joseph's jealous brothers had sold him as a slave, they plotted a scheme to deceive their father, Jacob. Taking their brother's coat, they dipped it in goat's blood and presented it to Jacob, saying, "We have found this coat. See whether it is Joseph's coat or not."

What liars they were! They even pretended not to recognize Joseph's coat, so as to ward off all suspicion. When Jacob saw it, he was horrified. "A wild beast has devoured my son!" he cried. And tears of inconsolable grief streamed down his cheeks.

What a contrast the picture provides between the father's anguished face and the hard, sly, guilty faces of his sons!

A lie is a word or an act by which one expresses the contrary of what he thinks or wills, usually with the intention to deceive others.

Lying is never permissible, not even for a good purpose, because it is intrinsically wrong and opposed to the natural law.

Lying undermines mutual trust among men, whereas the virtue of truthfulness promotes the general welfare of society.

God has given us speech that we may express our thoughts with sincerity and truth.

To the Lord, who is Truth, lying lips are an abomination.

**"Put away lying and speak truth each one with his neighbor, because we are members of one another."** Eph. 4:25

*Calumny* Botticelli-Alinari

***What does the eighth commandment of God, "Thou shalt not bear false witness against thy neighbor," forbid?***

**The eighth commandment of God forbids...rash judgment, detraction, calumny, and the telling of secrets we are bound to keep.**

Man possesses a treasure that is priceless, at times more precious than life itself: **honor.** God has protected this supreme good with the eighth commandment, which forbids the **defamation** of our neighbor.

A person injures his neighbor's honor by **backbiting,** by **malicious gossip,** and especially, by **calumniating** or slandering him, that is, falsely charging him with defects or sins.

The admirable art of Botticelli has given us an allegorical representation of **Calumny.** The sorrowful scene has the open sea as its background. To the right appears the judgment seat, and for the judge the artist has chosen King Midas who, according to mythology had the ears of a donkey, because he judged unjustly in a contest between the gods. Two grim figures, **Suspicion** and **Deceit,** are shouting into his donkey's ears perfidious insinuations designed to dissuade him from the truth, while **Calumny,** in the center of the picture, approaches dressed in white, the color of innocence, dragging by the hair the slandered one, who is imploring mercy. **Hatred** precedes, represented by a hooded man with a sinister aspect. Two charming girls, the **Falsehoods,** are crowning Calumny with flowers to give her a lovely appearance that the judge may be more readily deceived. A dark, ghastly figure follows behind; it is **Remorse,** which will never cease to pursue the calumniator.

**"The whisperer and the double tongued is accursed: for he has troubled many that were at peace."** Eccl. 28:15

***What must a person do who has sinned by detraction or calumny, or has told a secret he is bound to keep?***

**A person who has sinned by detraction or calumny, or who has told a secret he is bound to keep must repair the harm he has done to his neighbor, as far as he is able.**

*Esther Confounds Haman* By kind permission of Publ. Garzanti. From the Holy Bible

The Biblical story of Esther presents an example of a calumniator's punishment.

Proud, haughty Haman, prime minister of the king of Persia, was furious with a pious and just Jew, Mordecai, because he refused to worship him. He swore that he would destroy him and all the Jews in the kingdom. So he resorted to calumny. "There is a group of people in your kingdom," he said to the king, "who despise your orders. It is not expedient for you to let them grow insolent. Decree their destruction!"

The decree of condemnation was published in every part of the land. The cries of the Israelites reached heaven. Mordecai begged Esther the Queen, who was also a Jew, to save her people. Consequently, after having prayed and fasted, the beautiful Esther invited the king and Haman to a banquet and then with regal firmness, unmasked the calumniator. "My people and I have been handed over to our enemies to be killed," she declared. "Who is responsible for this?" demanded the king angrily. "Our adversary," answered Esther, "is this wicked Haman." Her words struck terror into the heart of the minister. He realized that his end had come. In fact, that day he paid for his sin with his life.

How wise are they who make it a practice never to speak of a person unless they can say something good of him! And how important it is to remember that the calumniator and he who makes known the hidden faults of another, without good reason, are obliged to repair the harm as far as they are able.

**"If we say less than we should it is easy to add, but having said too much it is hard to take it off."**

St. Francis de Sales

*The Family* Zarnardelli-Alinari

***What are we commanded by the ninth commandment of God, "Thou shalt not covet thy neighbor's wife"?***

**By the ninth commandment we are commanded to be pure in thought and desire.**

Observe this little family in the blissful peace of their humble home. The Christian home is the sanctuary of Christian love.

Only they who are pure in thought and desire can know the blessings of true love and the peace of God in their hearts.

Interior purity requires strength and resolution. Anyone can be impure, but it takes courage to be pure. The Patriarch Joseph in the holy Bible chose to face a false accusation and a prison sentence rather than stain his purity. Another Biblical figure, Susanna, the beautiful and holy wife of Joakim, also faced death rather than give in to the wicked desires of two old men, judges of the people, who had perverted their own minds so as not to remember the commandments of God. When they tempted her to sin, threatening to calumniate her if she should refuse, Susanna sighed, and said, "It is better for me to fall into your hands without doing this evil, than to sin in the sight of the Lord." She was condemned to death on the strength of the evil judges' testimony, as she had expected, but in answer to her prayer, God sent the prophet Daniel to expose the wickedness of the old men and thus, to save her life.

God is purity itself, and He wants us pure in mind, will, and heart. Moreover, by prohibiting the desire for another's wife, God requires the greatest respect for the family, for the bond of holy matrimony.

**"Love celestial desires, and desire celestial love."** St. Francis de Sales

*St. John the Baptist Accuses Herod* Fattori-Alinari

***What is forbidden by the ninth commandment of God, "Thou shalt not covet thy neighbor's wife"?***

**The ninth commandment forbids all thoughts and desires contrary to chastity.**

We are not responsible for impure thoughts which come into our minds **unbidden.** A mere temptation to impurity, even if accompanied by bodily feeling is like a spark falling on our clothes: it can do no harm if we brush it off quickly. The stronger the temptation a person has, the more merit he gains by resisting.

Thoughts about impure things become sinful when a person thinks of an unchaste act and deliberately takes pleasure in so thinking, or when an unchaste desire or passion is aroused and consent is given to it.

Internal sins are the source of external sins. "For out of the heart," said our Lord, "come evil thoughts, adulteries, immorality..." (Mt. 15:19).

The infamous King Herod, of whom we read in the Gospel, took for himself his brother's wife, Herodias. For this sin, he was sternly reproved by St. John the Baptist. "It is not lawful for you to have her," declared the saint.

The best way to resist impure thoughts and desires is by avoiding all unnecessary dangers, mortifying the senses, ignoring the temptation, occupying oneself, diverting one's mind to other things, and having immediate recourse to our Blessed Mother.

**"Do not say that you have chaste minds if you have unchaste eyes, because an unchaste eye is the messenger of an unchaste heart."**

St. Augustine

**"Occupy your minds with good thoughts, or the enemy will fill them with bad ones: unoccupied they cannot be."** St. Thomas More

*Ahab and Naboth* T. M. Roche-Ed. Sonzogno

***What does the tenth commandment of God, "Thou shalt not covet thy neighbor's goods," forbid?***

**The tenth commandment forbids all desire to take or to keep unjustly what belongs to others, and also forbids envy at their success.**

The holy Bible narrates the story of a covetous king, Ahab of Samaria, and Naboth, a man who owned a vineyard near the royal palace.

Greatly desirous of that vineyard, Ahab went to his subject and said, "Give me your vineyard that I may make a garden." Naboth, however, refused to relinquish the land of his fathers, his inheritance. When Jezebel, Ahab's wife, learned of the king's anger and bitterness over the refusal he had received, she contrived to have Naboth killed. Then she told her husband that he could take possession of the vineyard.

For this crime, the infamous couple were severely punished by God, who sent the Prophet Elijah to tell them: "You have slain; moreover, you have also taken possession. The dogs licked the blood of Naboth; they shall lick your blood also."

The tenth commandment forbids us to desire, to take or keep unjustly the property of others, and it also forbids envy at their success.

We must be content with what we have and with the conditions in which God has placed us. However, it is permissible to seek to become prosperous, if it is done honestly, and without exposing one's self to the proximate dangers of sin.

**"Covetousness is the root of all evils, and some in their eagerness to get rich have strayed from the faith and have involved themselves in many troubles."**
1 Tm. 6:10

**"Take heed and guard yourself from all covetousness, for a man's life does not consist in the abundance of his possessions."** Lk. 12:15

*The Theological Virtues* Tiepolo-Alinari

***What are the three theological virtues?***
**The three theological virtues are faith, hope, and charity.**

A virtue is a permanent disposition of the soul to do good and to avoid evil.

There are **natural virtues,** that is, good habits that even the unbelievers and pagans can acquire by frequent repetition of the same act. Then there are the **supernatural virtues** possessed by the justified. They are supernatural habits. Having been elevated to the supernatural order, we are given by God at Baptism supernatural powers, which enable us to perform supernatural acts.

The supernatural virtues are **faith, hope** and **charity,** allegorically represented in the illustration.

**Faith** is represented standing erect, clothed in light, humble but fearless. She is veiled because she believes the mysteries of God without understanding them. She is leaning on the cross, which recalls the mystery of redemption, and in her right hand, she is holding up the chalice, symbol of the mystery of the Holy Eucharist.

**Hope** is dressed in green, the color of springtime, and she is carrying an anchor. As an anchor holds a ship securely in the sea, so hope anchors the Christian soul securely in God.

**Charity** is wearing a golden dress. She is holding one poor infant close to her breast and another by the hand—a pose symbolic of her chaste and generous love.

Without faith, hope and charity, it is impossible to attain salvation.

**"Faith makes us know God; hope makes us look forward to joining Him; charity makes us His friends."** St. Thomas Aquinas

*The Canaanite* Palma-Alinari

***What is faith?***

**Faith is the virtue by which we firmly believe all the truths God has revealed, because God has revealed them, who can neither deceive nor be deceived.**

While our Lord was preaching one day, a poor Canaanite woman stepped out of the crowd and begged Him to cure her sick daughter. Jesus, however, answered her not a word. Nevertheless, the pagan woman insistently cried, "Lord, help me!" And Jesus answered, "It is not fair to take the children's bread and cast it to the dogs." Yet the woman replied humbly and confidently, "Yes, Lord, for even the dogs eat of the crumbs that fall from their masters' table." Then Jesus said to her, "O woman, great is your faith! Let it be done to you as you will!" And her daughter was cured instantly.

Faith is the virtue by which we firmly believe on the word of God all that He has revealed and teaches us through the Church.

We believe men in human affairs; we should not find it difficult to believe God, even in matters we cannot understand, since God, who is Truth itself, can neither deceive nor be deceived.

Faith is infused into our souls at Baptism. Without faith we cannot please God; only he who believes will be saved.

**"Human reason is weak, and may be deceived, but true faith cannot be deceived."**

Imitation of Christ

**"The man of faith shall be blessed with faithful Abraham."** Gal. 3:9

***What is hope?***

**Hope is the virtue by which we firmly trust that God, who is all-powerful and faithful to His promises, will in His mercy, give us eternal happiness and the means to obtain it.**

*The Martyrdom of St. Alexander* Loverini-Anderson

Our merciful Lord has made magnificent promises to those who observe His commandments: He has promised to share with them His everlasting happiness in heaven, and to give them all the graces necessary to attain to this supreme bliss.

We place our complete hope in God, because He is infinitely good, powerful, and faithful to His promises.

The one who despairs of his salvation supremely offends God.

A person proves his hope in God by not allowing the difficulties and trials of life to overcome him, and by being resigned to God's will always, trusting in His loving care.

The martyred soldier in the illustration is St. Alexander, who was beheaded for refusing to deny his Faith. Like all the glorious martyrs of the Church, he was certain of the crown of glory awaiting him in heaven.

It is true that the road to heaven is narrow, but we trust in the merits of Jesus Christ, who died for love of us.

**"I could never hope for pardon or heaven when I think of my great sins, but I venture to hope that through the merits of Christ I may be saved by means of penance and keeping of the commandments."** St. Augustine

**"God is never sought in vain, and when He is sought with hope, He is always found."** St. Bernard

*True Charity* Nicolo Sanesi-Alinari

***What is charity?***

**Charity is the virtue by which we love God above all things for His own sake, and our neighbor as ourselves for the love of God.**

When one of the Scribes asked Jesus which was the first commandment of all, our Lord answered, "The first commandment of all is: You shall love the Lord your God with your whole heart, and with your whole soul, and with your whole mind, and with your whole strength. And the second is like it: You shall love your neighbor as yourself" (Mk. 12:29-32).

We are first commanded to love God above all things. To love God above all things means to be willing to renounce every created thing rather than offend God by mortal sin. We do not need to **feel** more love for God than for men, for love is essentially a matter of the will, not of the feelings.

We are also commanded to love our neighbor as ourselves for the love of God. Our neighbor includes all living human beings, even our enemies. St. John wrote, "If anyone says, 'I love God,' and hates his brother, he is a liar. For how can he who does not love his brother, whom he sees, love God, whom he does not see?" (1 Jn. 4:20)

To love means to do good or at least to desire to do so. In the illustration, the good friar giving bread to the destitute beggar, although poor himself, is willing to offer what help he can to one who is poorer.

**"He who knows by experience how sweet and delightful it is to love God, loses all taste for earthly things."** St. Alphonsus

**"Charity to our neighbor is more pleasing to God than solitude and pious thoughts."** St. Teresa

***What are moral virtues?***

**Moral virtues are virtues which dispose us to lead moral, or good lives by aiding us to treat persons and things in the right way, that is, according to the will of God.**

***What is the virtue of religion?***

**Religion is the highest moral virtue; it disposes us to offer to God the worship that is due Him.**

*The Faith and Sacrifice of the Ancient Law* — Veronese-Anderson

We belong to God; we owe Him our very existence. It is our duty to **know, love,** and **serve** our Creator. Religion is the virtue by which we fulfill this fundamental obligation of worshiping God.

In the magnificent picture by Paul Veronese, **Religion** is represented allegorically by a feminine figure drawing attention to the veiled chalice she holds aloft. That chalice contains our hidden God, in the adorable Sacrament of the Holy Eucharist, the center of Christian worship.

Religion unites us intimately to God, inclining our hearts to adoration, thanksgiving and prayer.

The divine virtue of religion has been championed by the greatest men of all ages, practiced by apostles and martyrs in the catacombs, by dedicated men and women in monasteries and convents, by kings and Sovereign Pontiffs in magnificent cathedrals, by valiant soldiers on the battlefield, by learned scholars in great centers of culture, by the masses of working people in parish churches the world over, and by exemplary families in the intimacy of their homes.

Religion is the foundation of every true moral order. A moral code which is not founded on religion is nothing but an empty word.

**"A man who is religious, is religious morning, noon, and night; his religion is a certain character, a mold in which his thoughts, words, and actions are cast, all forming parts of one and the same whole."**

Cardinal Newman

*Prudence* Tiepolo-Alinari

***What is prudence?***

**Prudence is the virtue which disposes us in all circumstances to form right judgments about what we must or must not do.**

We were created for heaven. Our earthly life is a preparation for it. A prudent person always reflects and chooses the means best suited to help him reach his eternal destiny.

How expressive is Tiepolo's allegorical representation of Prudence! She is standing like a sentinel, with her gaze fixed on heaven, her ultimate goal. From heaven comes the light which enlightens and guides her along the path of virtue. Entwined about her right arm is a serpent, symbolic of prudence. "Be wise as serpents," exhorted our Lord (Mt. 10:16). When sensing danger, a serpent will expose its body but protect its head. Likewise, the prudent Christian will rather risk his life than lose his soul.

In her left hand, Prudence carries a mirror, because before acting, a prudent person intently examines every aspect of the proposed action in the mirror of reason lit by faith. She looks at things calmly; she judges them rightly, foresees difficulties and takes the proper precautions. Not trusting her own judgment, she asks the advice of the wise, and thus she walks unhesitatingly and confidently on the road to sanctity.

The saints were models of prudence. They realized full well how short life is, and they made good use of their time. Before deciding to do a thing, they would ask themselves, "How will this serve me for eternity?" They would then act accordingly.

**"See to it, brethren, that you walk with care: not as unwise, but as wise, making the most of your time, and understand what the will of the Lord is."**

Eph. 5:15

***What is justice?***

**Justice is the virtue which disposes us to give everyone what belongs to him.**

One day, the tax collectors of the temple approached Saint Peter to ask, "Does your Master not pay the didrachma?"

"Yes," answered Peter. But, when he entered the house, Jesus spoke first. He told Peter, "Go to the sea, and cast a hook; and take the first fish that comes up. And opening its mouth you shall find a stater; take that and give it to them for me and for you."

Jesus was just. He respected the rights of others, obeyed the authorities and paid lawful taxes.

"Justice," says St. Thomas, "is a certain rectitude of mind whereby a man does what is right in the circumstances confronting him."

*Jesus Commands that Tribute Be Paid* Spagnoletto-Alinari

A man who is just gives to God due worship; to his country, loyalty; to his parents, honor and obedience, and to his fellowman, brotherly love and respect—respect for his right to life and freedom, to the sanctity of his home, to his good name and honor, and to his external possessions.

Jesus called the just blessed: "Blessed are they who hunger and thirst for justice: for they shall be satisfied" (Mt. 5:6). They are blessed on earth and rewarded in heaven, as was St. Joseph, whom the holy Gospel calls a **just man.**

**"Render to all men whatever is their due; tribute to whom tribute is due; taxes to whom taxes are due; fear to whom fear is due; honor to whom honor is due."**

Rom. 13:7

*The Martyrdom of St. Lawrence* Grandi-Alinari

***What is fortitude?***

**Fortitude is the virtue which disposes us to do what is good in spite of any difficulty.**

St. Lawrence was one of the deacons dedicated to the service of the Church of Rome. Much beloved of Pope Sixtus II, he had been placed by the Sovereign Pontiff in charge of administering the goods of the Church and distributing its revenue to the poor. During the terrible persecution enforced by the Emperor Valerian, the Pope was arrested and led away to be executed. Lawrence followed him weeping. "Do not grieve for me," said the Pontiff. "A more painful martyrdom is reserved for you. Within five days you will follow me."

St. Lawrence prepared himself by distributing to the poor everything over which he had charge. Thus, when the Prefect of Rome ordered him to hand over the treasures of the Church, the holy deacon brought him a pitiful band of old people, invalids, lepers, orphans and widows. Enraged, the Prefect ordered him to be stretched out on a gridiron and slowly burned to death. What horrible torture! And yet, the saint rejoiced. What heroic fortitude!

The virtue of fortitude is not to be confused with physical strength.

He who possesses the virtue of fortitude keeps his passions under control, resists temptations, overcomes vain human respect and, when necessary, prudently and courageously faces every trial and danger, even death itself, for the service of God and the good of his neighbor.

**A man gives proof of strength of character and courage in the highest degree when he bears serenely and without complaint the tribulations God permits for his sanctification.**

***What is temperance?***

**Temperance is the virtue which disposes us to control our desires and to use rightly the things which please our senses.**

King David was once tortured by thirst when encamped with his armies in a place where there was no water to be had. Consequently, three of his most valiant men risked their lives to cross the enemy line and fetch water from a distant fountain. However, when they presented it in a helmet to David, he exclaimed, "I shall not drink the blood of my courageous men!" Whereupon, he poured the water out on the ground, offering it as a sacrifice to the Lord.

*Thirsty King David Makes a Sacrifice of Water* Schnorr

David's action is a beautiful example of temperance.

Temperance is the virtue which restrains our desires for things which please our senses, especially food, repose and amusements. If a person seeks inordinate pleasure in these things, he runs the risk of making them the end purpose of his life. The Christian must have control over himself and regulate his entire life with reason and faith.

In imitation of our Lord Jesus Christ, who subjected Himself to penance, and in accordance with His exhortation to mortification, the Church prescribes for the faithful the law of fast and abstinence on certain days during Lent. The time of Lent preserves its penitential character.... Abstinence is to be observed on every Friday of Lent, while abstinence and fast are to be observed on Ash Wednesday and Good Friday (see Apostolic Constitution on Fast and Abstinence). The Church commands us to fast and abstain also in order that we may control the desires of the flesh, raise our minds more freely to God, and make satisfaction for sin.

A mortified person prays better, and his prayers are more quickly answered. Moreover, it is a historical fact that nations which have practiced penance and prayer have obtained mercy and forgiveness from God.

**"Prayer is good with fasting and alms more than to lay up treasures of gold."** Tb. 12:8

PART III

# THE SACRAMENTS AND GRACE

***What is grace?***

**Grace is a supernatural gift of God bestowed on us through the merits of Jesus Christ for our salvation.**

Wearied from a journey, Jesus was resting one noon by Jacob's well near the city of Sichar, in Samaria. His disciples had gone into the city to buy some food. A Samaritan woman approached to draw water, and Jesus asked her for a drink. The woman replied, "How is it that you, although you are a Jew, ask a drink of me, who am a Samaritan woman?" At that time the Jews did not associate with Samaritans. "If you did know the gift of God," answered the Savior, "and who it is who says to you, 'Give me to drink,' you, perhaps, would have asked of him, and he would have given you living water."

The living water that Jesus offered the Samaritan woman was His divine **grace.**

Grace is a supernatural gift of God which confers on our souls a new life, that is, a sharing in the life of God Himself. It makes us holy and pleasing to God and gives us the right to heaven. It makes us adopted children of God and temples of the Holy Spirit.

What transforming power the grace of God possesses! "As soon as grace appears in a soul," wrote Cornelius A' Lapide, S.J., "it weeps for its faults, abandons itself with resignation to God, and burns with celestial love. Then the mountains of pride begin to liquify; the torrents of vanity and ambition disappear; the flames of impurity become ice; laziness, fear and sloth vanish."

With the Samaritan woman, let us cry out to the Lord:

**"Give me this water (divine grace) that I may not thirst."** Jn. 4:15

*The Samaritan Woman* Dorè-Garzanti

*Jesus Sends His Apostles To Preach* Schnorr

***What is a sacrament?***

**A sacrament is an outward sign instituted by Christ to give grace.**

"All power in heaven and on earth has been given to me," our Lord told His Apostles before He ascended into heaven. "Go, therefore, and make disciples of all nations, baptizing them in the name of the Father, and of the Son, and of the Holy Spirit, teaching them to observe all that I have commanded you; and behold, I am with you all days, even unto the consummation of the world" (Mt. 28:18-20). Jesus addressed these words not only to the first Apostles, who would die, but also to their successors, that is, to the Pope and to the bishops. And in truth, the Church has never ceased to teach, convert and sanctify in every age. Indeed, the better to fulfill its divine commission, it has divided the faithful into dioceses and parishes and obliged bishops and pastors to reside therein, that the faithful may not only be instructed in the Faith, but may also have the opportunity to receive the sacraments, which give the grace we need to observe all that God and the Church command.

The sacraments were instituted by Christ to sanctify the most important events of our whole life and provide for our every spiritual need.

Christ willed that the sacraments be administered by men who act in His name. Yet the sacraments receive from God, through the merits of Jesus Christ, their power to give grace. They always give grace if received with the right dispositions.

**The sacraments are gifts of the infinite mercy of God. Let us use them for the purpose God had in instituting them: to help us on our way to salvation.**

*The Kiss of Judas* Dorè-Garzanti

***What sin does one commit who knowingly receives a sacrament of the living in mortal sin?***

**He who knowingly receives a sacrament of the living in mortal sin commits a mortal sin of sacrilege, because he treats a sacred thing with grave irreverence.**

When, after the Last Supper, our divine Lord was praying in the Garden of Gethsemane, His enemies came armed with swords and clubs to take Him prisoner. The traitorous apostle Judas was at their head, leading the way. In the eerie light of their torches, the villains beheld the divinely majestic figure of Christ. Trembling, Judas approached Him. "Hail, Master," he cried, and going nearer, kissed Him.

How loathsome was that traitor's kiss! On the lips of Judas, love's purest expression became a treacherous sign of betrayal. Wretched Judas! How much better it would have been for him had he never been born!

A person commits an equally outrageous act who approaches a sacrament of the living knowing that he is not in God's grace. The **sacraments of the living** are Confirmation, Holy Eucharist, Anointing of the Sick, Holy Orders and Matrimony. These sacraments should be received by souls spiritually alive through sanctifying grace. Their chief purpose is to give more grace. It is a sacrilege to receive one of these sacraments in the state of mortal sin.

Baptism and Penance, on the other hand, are called sacraments of the dead because their chief purpose is to give the life of sanctifying grace to souls spiritually dead through sin.

Before receiving the sacraments, let us arouse sentiments of faith and reverence, thinking of the sacredness of that which we are about to receive.

**"If our hearts were prepared as they might and ought to be by contrition and piety, the grace of even one Communion would suffice to sanctify us in body, soul, and spirit."**

Cardinal Manning

*Jesus and Nicodemus* Schnorr

***What is Baptism?***

**Baptism is the sacrament that gives our souls the new life of sanctifying grace by which we become children of God and heirs of heaven.**

A certain Pharisee named Nicodemus, a learned, cultured man highly esteemed by all, went to Jesus at night for the sake of secrecy. "Rabbi," he said, "we know that you are a teacher from God, for no one can work these signs that you work unless God be with him." Nicodemus believed Jesus to be a Prophet, or perhaps even the Messiah come to found God's new kingdom. Being a descendant of Abraham, he may have hoped to obtain one of the first places in this kingdom. But Jesus answered: "Amen, amen, I say to you, unless a man be born again, he cannot see the kingdom of God."

"How can a man be born again when he is old?" Nicodemus objected. And the Divine Master said, **"Unless a man be born again of water and the Spirit, he cannot enter into the kingdom of God."**

With these words, our Lord explained the manner by which men were to be born into the supernatural life of grace, by means of water and the Holy Spirit; that is, through **holy Baptism.** Hence, the **absolute necessity** of holy Baptism for all—if not Baptism by water, then Baptism by desire or blood to enter into the kingdom of God.

Baptism purifies the soul from every sin, original and actual; it infuses in it sanctifying grace, thus creating a new man: a Christian, a child of God and an heir of heaven.

**"For Christians, there are two births: one, earthly and the other, heavenly; one of the flesh, the other of the spirit; one of a father and mother, the other of God and the Church."** St. Augustine

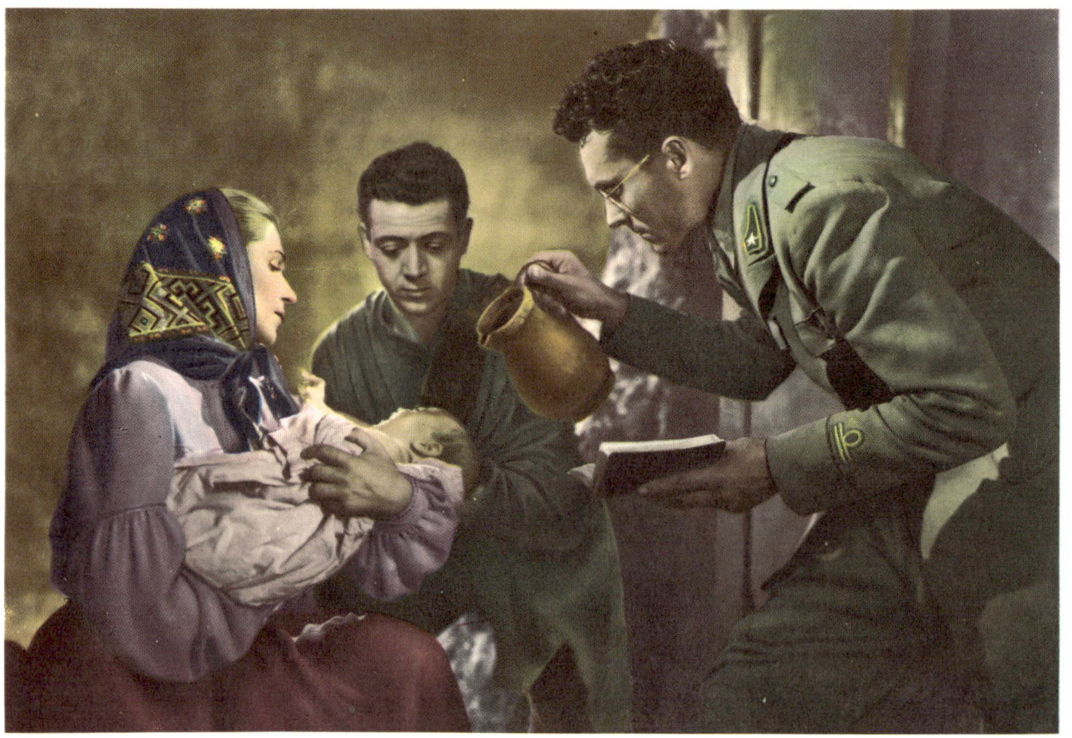

*Baptism on the Battle Field* From Man of the Cross

***How would you give Baptism?***

**I would give Baptism by pouring ordinary water on the forehead of the person to be baptized, saying while pouring it: "I baptize you in the name of the Father, and of the Son, and of the Holy Spirit."**

While enemy planes screamed through the skies, raining fire upon a certain European city, during World War II, a baby was born in a small cottage in which a group of soldiers had taken shelter. The infant was so frail that death seemed imminent. It was urgent that the baby be baptized, but no priest could be had at such a time. The lieutenant in command, therefore, took a pitcher and poured water on the child's forehead, while saying the words of the form, "I baptize you...."

The priest is the usual minister of Baptism, having received the power to baptize from Jesus Christ Himself. However, in times of necessity, when a priest is unavailable, anyone, even a heretic or an unbaptized person, may and should baptize. If he performs the ceremony correctly and has the intention of doing what the Church does, the Baptism is valid.

Because Baptism is necessary for salvation, children should be baptized as soon as reasonably possible after birth.

Those chosen as godparents for Baptism should be good, practicing Catholics since it is their duty to see to it that the child be brought up a good Catholic, if this is not done by the parents.

The name of a saint is given in Baptism in order that the person baptized may imitate his virtues and have him for a protector.

**"I will greatly rejoice in the Lord, for he has clothed me with the garments of salvation; and with the robe of justice he has covered me."**

Is. 61:10

***What is Confirmation?***

**Confirmation is the sacrament through which the Holy Spirit comes to us in a special way and enables us to profess our Faith as strong and perfect Christians and soldiers of Jesus Christ.**

It was Pentecost, the fiftieth day after Easter. Gathered in the Cenacle together with the pious women and Mary, the Mother of Jesus, the Apostles prayed as they waited for the descent of the Holy Spirit promised by the Master. "And suddenly there came a sound from heaven, as of a violent wind blowing, and it filled the whole house where they were sitting. And there appeared to them parted tongues as of fire, which settled upon each of them. And they were all filled with the Holy Spirit and began to speak in foreign tongues, even as the Holy Spirit prompted them to speak."

*Pentecost* Titian-Alinari

In this painting of the great event by the master, Titian, beams of light stream down from the mystical Dove on high, a symbol of the Holy Spirit. The Apostles and the pious women are gathered around Mary, their Queen.

The descent of the Holy Spirit completely transformed the Apostles. From poor, ignorant, weak, and timid fishermen, they became teachers of the world, fearless preachers of Jesus Christ. And all of them crowned their zealous labors of love with martyrdom.

Confirmation produces similar effects in those souls who receive it with the proper dispositions, and who cooperate with the grace of this sacrament, through which the Holy Spirit comes to us in a special way and enables us to profess our Faith as more mature followers of Christ.

Confirmation increases sanctifying grace and gives us the strength we need to overcome the dangers to salvation. It also imprints a lasting character on our soul, and infuses in it in greater abundance the gifts of the Holy Spirit.

**"The sacrament which gives strength to those who are reborn by Baptism is for those who would fight for Christ."** St. Thomas Aquinas

*St. Sebastian* Sodoma-Alinari

***What does the sacramental grace of Confirmation help us to do?***

**The sacramental grace of Confirmation helps us to live our Faith loyally and to profess it courageously.**

How many masterpieces the dramatic martyrdom of Saint Sebastian has inspired! Observe him in the present picture, bound to a tree, the target of the bowmen's arrows. His gaze is fixed on heaven, where a crown of immortal glory awaits him. His expression betrays the agony he is suffering with marvelous courage, while offering his bleeding body to his Creator as a precious holocaust. Left there to die, Sebastian was found and cared for by the Christians. When he had regained sufficient strength, the fearless saint presented himself to the Emperor Diocletian and, pointing to his livid scars, denounced his inhumanly cruel treatment of Christians. Whereupon, the enraged persecutor had him clubbed to death.

Sebastian was a Roman soldier. In fact, he was a captain of the praetorian guard. He served his emperor faithfully, but his first allegiance was to his God.

Every Christian must serve courageously under the banner of Christ.

**Confirmation** is the sacrament which helps us become perfect Christians, to live our Faith loyally and to profess and defend it courageously even at the cost of our lives. Confirmation, in fact, adds to the grace of Baptism a special grace which enables us to wage war against the three great enemies of our salvation: the world, the flesh and the devil.

It is well to receive the Sacrament of Confirmation at the age when a child becomes a youth, because the strength it gives is needed to resist the many temptations surrounding him at that period.

**"You shall receive power when the Holy Spirit comes upon you, and you shall be witnesses for me in Jerusalem, and in all Judea, and Samaria, and even to the very ends of the earth."** Acts 1:8

***What is necessary to receive Confirmation properly?***

**To receive Confirmation properly it is necessary to be in the state of grace, and to know well the chief truths and duties of our religion.**

*Confirmation* Crespi

In administering Confirmation, the bishop extends his hands over those who are to be confirmed, prays that they may receive the Holy Spirit, and, anoints the forehead of each candidate with holy chrism in the form of a cross.

He calls the person by name and prays that he or she receive the Holy Spirit, Gift of the Father.

The holy chrism is a mixture of olive oil and balm. Olive oil, once used to strengthen the limbs of athletes, signifies the strengthening grace of Confirmation. Balm, a fragrant preservative, signifies the sweetness of virtue and freedom from the corruption of sin.

The anointing with holy chrism in the form of a cross signifies that we must always be ready to profess our Faith openly and to practice it fearlessly.

The candidate for Confirmation must be well instructed in the chief truths and duties of our religion and approach the sacrament in the state of grace. Furthermore, he must have as his sponsor, a baptized and confirmed Catholic.

After having been confirmed, the Catholic should continue to study his religion, so that he may be able to explain and defend it.

**"We who are confirmed are signed with the cross of Christ. We are enrolled by bishops, who are like the leaders in Christ's army: the imposition of hands reminds us that virtue and strength come from Christ."**

St. Thomas Aquinas

*The Redeemer* Dolci-Alinari

***What is the Holy Eucharist?***

**The Holy Eucharist is a sacrament and a sacrifice. In the Holy Eucharist under the appearances of bread and wine, the Lord Christ is contained, offered, and received.**

Jesus, "having loved his own who were in the world, loved them to the end!" (Jn. 13:1) The night before He died, while men were plotting to betray Him, He gathered His Apostles together for a sublime love feast. And at that Last Supper, He instituted the sacrament which is the greatest gift of His most loving heart.

Behold Christ at the solemn moment of the institution of the Holy Eucharist. His divine face reflects the infinite goodness of His heart, and His right hand is raised in blessing.

Christ instituted the Holy Eucharist in this way: He took bread, blessed and broke it, and giving it to His Apostles, said: "Take and eat; this is my Body"; then He took a cup of wine, blessed it, and giving it to them, said: "All of you drink of this; for this is my Blood, the Blood of the new covenant which is being shed for many unto the forgiveness of sins"; finally He gave His Apostles the commission: "Do this in remembrance of me" (cf. Mt. 26:26-28; Lk. 22:19).

When our Lord said, "This is my Body," the entire substance of the bread was changed into His Body; and when He said, "This is my Blood," the entire substance of the wine was changed into His Blood.

Christ could not have used clearer, more explicit words. He did not say, "This is a symbol of my Body," or "This represents my Body," but "This **is** my Body." We take Christ at His word, because He is God. He is able to change bread and wine into His Body and Blood by His almighty power.

**"I am the bread of life. If anyone eat of this bread he shall live forever; and the bread that I will give is my flesh for the life of the world."**

John 6:48-52

***Is the same Jesus Christ present in the Holy Eucharist who is in heaven and who was born on earth of the Blessed Virgin Mary?***

**The same Jesus Christ who is in heaven and was born on earth of the Blessed Virgin Mary is present in the Holy Eucharist.**

*The Eucharist* M. Traverso

In this moving scene, full of light and color, our Lord in the Blessed Sacrament is surrounded by loving hearts. Nearest to the sacred Host is a band of radiant angels joining with men in singing hymns of adoration and love. Kneeling at the foot of the altar is St. Anthony Mary Zachary, a most zealous promoter of the Forty Hours Devotion. With him are devout faithful from every walk of life. Their faces, each with its own expression, mirror the sentiments filling their souls. Most captivating of all is the infant blowing kisses and stretching out his tiny hand toward Him who said, "Let the little children come unto me."

Our eyes, too, are drawn toward the sacred Host. Although we cannot see Christ with our bodily eyes in this sacrament, we are certain of His presence because we have His word for it. Nothing is truer than the word of Truth itself. Therefore, we believe that the Lord Jesus is really, truly and substantially present in the Holy Eucharist: that same Jesus whom the Virgin Mary bore in her womb and embraced in her arms, who was crucified for us, rose triumphantly from the dead, and reigns gloriously in heaven.

In the Holy Eucharist the whole Christ is present, Body, Blood, Soul, and Divinity.

**"When you see the Body of Christ exposed, say to yourself: This is that Body which was once covered with blood, pierced by a lance, from which issued saving fountains upon the world, one of blood and the other of water.... This Body He gave to us to keep and to eat, as a mark of His intense love."**

St. John Chrysostom

*The Miracle at Bolsena* Raphael-Alinari

***Is Jesus Christ whole and entire both under the appearances of bread and under the appearances of wine?***

**Jesus Christ is whole and entire both under the appearances of bread and under the appearances of wine.**

A German priest on a pilgrimage to Rome in 1263 stopped to celebrate Mass in the city of Bolsena. For some time he had been tormented by an agonizing doubt as to whether Jesus was truly present in the consecrated Host.... That same doubt was in his mind as he consecrated the bread and wine that morning. But while he was breaking the Host over the chalice, it suddenly began to drip blood as if it were living flesh. "A miracle!" cried the people.

Christ gave His priests the power to change bread and wine into His Body and Blood when He made the Apostles priests at the Last Supper by saying to them: "Do this in remembrance of me" (Lk. 22:19). Priests exercise their power to change bread and wine into the Body and Blood of Christ by repeating at the consecration of the Mass the words of Christ: "This is my body.... This is my blood."

After the words of the consecration, there is no longer any bread or wine on the altar, for they have been changed into our Lord's Body and Blood; there remain only the appearances of bread and wine.

Christ is whole and entire both under the appearances of bread and under the appearances of wine for since He can die no more, His Blood is forever united to His Body.

**"Does any unbeliever profess that the changing of bread and wine into the Body and Blood of the Lord is impossible? Then let him consider God's omnipotence."** St. Thomas Aquinas

*Adoration of the Eucharist* Ridolfi

***Why does Christ give us His own Body and Blood in the Holy Eucharist?***

**Christ gives us His own Body and Blood in the Holy Eucharist: to be offered as a sacrifice commemorating and renewing for all time the sacrifice of the cross; to be received by the faithful in Holy Communion; to remain ever on our altars as the proof of His love for us; and to be worshiped by us.**

Around the throne of the Eucharistic King are gathered loving adorers of widely-scattered nations, dressed in the colorful costumes of their people.

Our divine Lord loves every member of the human race so very much that He devised a means to be the intimate companion of each of His followers in every age and in every part of the earth. He is present in the Holy Eucharist to be the Friend and Brother of our souls, the comfort, strength and joy of our lives.

Every hour, somewhere in the world, Holy Mass is offered, and Jesus becomes Eucharistically present on the altar. Oh, how immense is the power and goodness of our God, who willed to be near all His children and unite them all with one bond of charity and fraternal unity.

The first sentiment of our hearts toward our Lord in the Blessed Sacrament should be profound adoration, since He is God. The next should be ardent love, for Jesus remains on our altars out of love for us.

We prove our love for Christ in the Holy Eucharist by hearing Mass and receiving Holy Communion as often as possible, by attending Benediction, by paying Him visits, by spending an hour in adoration when the Blessed Sacrament is exposed, and by other devotions.

**"Come to me, all you who labor and are burdened, and I will give you rest."** Mt. 11:28

*The Centurion* Veronese-Alinari

***What is Holy Communion?***

**Holy Communion is the receiving of Jesus Christ in the Sacrament of the Holy Eucharist. To receive Holy Communion worthily it is necessary to be free from mortal sin, to have a right intention, and to obey the Church's laws on the fast required before Holy Communion.**

A Roman centurion went to our Lord to beg Him to cure a much-loved servant. When Jesus replied with His customary kindness, "I will come and cure him," the centurion protested, "Lord, I am not worthy that you should come under my roof, but only say the word and my servant will be healed." His humility and great faith won the admiration of the Son of God.

Besides a soul free from mortal sin, Jesus wants to find dispositions of humility and faith in those who receive Him.

Venial sins do not prevent us from going to Holy Communion. But we shall receive more grace if we try to free ourselves from **deliberate** venial sin.

Out of respect for our Lord, the Church obliges us before receiving Holy Communion—whether in the morning, afternoon, evening, or at midnight Mass—to fast at least **one hour** from solid foods. This also applies to the consumption of alcoholic beverages, but in this case, even more moderation is recommended. Water may be taken **any time** before Holy Communion. The sick may take non-alcoholic drinks and medicine, **without any limit of time.**

The Eucharistic fast is not binding on those receiving Holy Viaticum.

**"In His mercy and grace, our Lord deigns to come to us in Holy Communion to give us new grace and to inflame us anew in the amendment of our defects. Let us prepare our hearts with devotion to receive our Beloved."**

Imitation of Christ

*Tobit and the Angel* Guardi-Fiortini

***How should we prepare ourselves for Holy Communion?***

**We should prepare ourselves for Holy Communion by thinking of our divine Redeemer whom we are about to receive, and by making fervent acts of faith, hope, love, and contrition.**

In Old Testament times, God showered the family of Tobit with blessings. He sent the Archangel Raphael to accompany their son on his successful journey from the city of Nineveh to Rages in Media.

"What can we offer this holy man by way of recompense?" wondered the father and son, their hearts full of gratitude toward him. They would have given him half of all they owned, but the Archangel refused saying, "Bless the God of heaven, give glory to Him, because He has shown His mercy to you." And having revealed himself, "he returned to Him who had sent him." Struck with amazement and awe, Tobit and his son fell prostrate and lay thus for three hours, blessing and thanking God.

We are far more privileged than Tobit, however, for in Holy Communion we receive, not an archangel, but the God of infinite majesty Himself, the Creator of heaven and earth, our Lord and Savior. We must prepare ourselves properly to receive Him, so that we may derive the full benefit of His visit. We should be devout and recollected, thinking of Jesus whom we are about to receive, and ardently desiring Him.

After Holy Communion we should spend some time adoring our Lord, thanking Him, renewing our promises of love and of obedience to Him, and asking Him for blessings for ourselves and others.

**"Remain in recollection after you have received your God and enjoy Him; for you possess Him whom all the world cannot take away from you."**

Imitation of Christ

*St. Palazia in Adoration* Guercino-Anderson

***What are the chief effects of a worthy Holy Communion?***

**The chief effects of a worthy Holy Communion are: a closer union with our Lord and a more fervent love of God and of our neighbor; an increase of sanctifying grace; preservation from mortal sin and the remission of venial sin; the lessening of our inclinations to sin and the help to practice good works.**

How beautiful is this painting by Guercino. Enraptured, the Christian soul contemplates the Holy Eucharist, that bread of eternal life which alone can satisfy man's ardent desire for God. Before Him who wraps all things in His heavenly light, the soul forgets every sorrow and every human attraction; it finds new energy and joyfully loses itself in Him who is infinite. Just as incense when it burns wraps the altar in fragrant clouds, so, too, he who gives himself totally to his God, to the divine Sanctifier, wholly consumes his life in a perpetual holocaust of faith and love.

**Holy Communion** increases sanctifying grace and all virtues in our soul. It closely unites us to the heart of Jesus and fills us with divine sweetness and greater love for God and neighbor. It purifies our soul and is Itself a pledge of eternal life.

The Holy Eucharist is the greatest of all sacraments. In fact, whereas we receive grace in the other sacraments, we receive here the very Author of grace.

**"This I ask for, this I desire, that by Holy Communion, I may unite myself entirely to You, detach my heart from all created things, and more and more learn to have a taste for heavenly and eternal things."**

Imitation of Christ

***When are we obliged to receive Holy Communion?***

**We are obliged to receive Holy Communion during Easter time each year and when in danger of death.**

*St. Jerome's Communion* Domenichino-Alinari

When after a life spent in study, solitude and austere penance, St. Jerome sensed that his death was near, he asked to be brought to the church near his hermitage to receive his last Holy Communion. Observe how Domenichino has depicted the great Doctor of the Church in that solemn moment. Fatigued by age and illness, he can no longer stand upright, but the ardor with which he looks upon the sacred Host reveals his profound faith and love. Raising his tired arms he seems to exclaim: "Come, Lord Jesus! Within a few hours, freed from this mortal body, I will no longer contemplate You beneath the Eucharistic veils, but in the full splendor of Your glory!"

The Holy Eucharist is the food of our soul. Our Lord made the reception of this sacrament a strict obligation for us, with the solemn warning: "Unless you eat the flesh of the Son of Man, and drink his blood, you shall not have life in you" (Jn. 6:53).

Carrying out the wishes of Jesus, the first Christians received Communion each time they assisted at Holy Mass. Later, when Christian piety lost some of its original fervor, the Church ruled that every faithful Catholic who has reached the age of reason must receive the Sacrament of the Eucharist at least once a year, during the Easter time, and also whenever in danger of death.

Christ in the Blessed Sacrament is the strength and light of all who work and struggle; He is the hope and protection of those about to cross the threshold of eternity. If it is important to begin life with the grace of God, it is not less important to close it with the mystic food which opens the gates of heaven.

**"He who eats my flesh and drinks my blood has life everlasting and I will raise him up on the last day."** John 6:54

*Elijah is Fed by the Angel* By kind permission of Publ. Garzanti. From the Holy Bible

***Why is it well to receive Holy Communion often, even daily?***

**It is well to receive Holy Communion often, even daily, because this intimate union with Jesus Christ, the Source of all holiness and the Giver of all graces, is the greatest aid to a holy life.**

Persecuted by the impious Queen Jezebel, the prophet Elijah fled into the desert and walked for a whole day without resting. Weary and disheartened, he finally threw himself down at the foot of a juniper tree and asked the Lord to let him die. But twice God sent an angel to bring him food and drink, and finally, strengthened by that food, the prophet walked for forty days and forty nights, until he reached the Mount of God, Horeb.

The miraculous bread which gave Elijah renewed courage and vigor was a type, a foreshadowing, of the Holy Eucharist, the true Bread of angels, by reason of which we are able to cross the wearisome desert of life with light hearts until we are admitted to the beatific vision of God in heaven.

By giving us His Body and Blood in the Holy Eucharist under the appearances of bread and wine, our Lord Jesus Christ wished us to understand that just as we nourish our bodies each day with bread, we should also nourish our souls with the Holy Eucharist, that we may be able to lead holy lives.

If a person is free from mortal sin, he can and should receive our Lord as often as possible. Christ did not intend the Eucharist to be a reward of virtue; He did not institute it for angels. He instituted it for men.

The fervent follower of Christ nourishes his soul with the Holy Eucharist daily, or if this is impossible, he receives every time he assists at Mass.

**"In every Communion, we are made flesh of His flesh, and bone of His bone; and if our hearts are pure, we are made also heart of His heart, mind of His mind, will of His will, spirit of His spirit."** Cardinal Manning

*What is the Mass?*

**The Mass is the sacrifice of the New Law in which Christ, through the ministry of the priest, offers Himself to God in an unbloody manner under the appearances of bread and wine.**

*Abraham and Melchizedek* L. Spada-Alinari

Since the dawn of the world, men have acknowledged their dependence on their Creator by offering sacrifices to Him, God Himself having taught them to do so. In the Holy Bible, we read of the offerings of Abel, the sacrifice of Noah, and Abraham's willingness to immolate his own son, Isaac, if God had desired it. The sacrifice offered by Melchizedek, however, was singular and very significant. When Abraham returned victorious from a battle against the heathen kings, Melchizedek blessed the Patriarch, and in thanksgiving offered God **an oblation of bread and wine.** This oblation is a very clear type of the Sacrifice of the Mass, in which Christ offers God the Father His own most precious Body and Blood, in an unbloody manner, under the appearances of bread and wine.

A **sacrifice** is the offering of a victim by a priest to God alone, and the destruction of it in some way to acknowledge that He is the Creator of all things. The various ancient sacrifices, either bloody or unbloody, were only figures of the Holy Sacrifice of the Mass. Through His prophet Malachi, God announced His intention to institute a new sacrifice: "From the rising of the sun even to the going down, my name is great among the Gentiles: and in every place there is sacrifice, and there is offered to my name a clean oblation" (Mal. 1:10-11).

This clean oblation, which is offered the world over to Almighty God, is the **Holy Sacrifice of the Mass,** in which Jesus Christ Himself, the Son of God, is the Victim.

**"There is no worthier oblation, no greater satisfaction for the washing away of sins, than to offer yourself purely and entirely to God, together with the oblation of the Body of Christ, in the Holy Mass."** Imitation of Christ

*Holy Mass* Catani-Anderson

***Who is the principal priest in every Mass?***

**The principal priest in every Mass is Jesus Christ, who offers to His heavenly Father, through the ministry of His ordained priest, His Body and Blood which were sacrificed on the cross.**

Jesus celebrated the first Holy Mass at the Last Supper when He said, "This is my body which is being **given for you.** This is my blood which is being **shed** for many unto the forgiveness of sins." At that very moment, He offered to the Father, the sacrifice of His sacred Body and His most precious Blood under the appearances of bread and wine, and the next day, He consummated that sacrifice by dying on the cross.

Holy Mass is the same sacrifice as the sacrifice of the cross because in the Mass the victim is the same, and the principal priest is the same—Jesus Christ. The **manner** in which the sacrifice is offered, however, is different. On the cross, Christ physically shed His Blood and was physically slain, while in the Mass there is no physical shedding of blood nor physical death, because Christ can die no more. On the cross Christ gained merit and satisfied for us, while in the Mass, He applies to us the merits and satisfaction of His death on the cross.

In Catani's expressive painting, the priest lifts the chalice of Christ's Blood to heaven, while at his side, an angel offers the Heavenly Father the sacrifices and petitions of the faithful, represented by the flowers gathered in his mantle.

The Mass is offered to adore God as our Creator and Lord; to thank Him for His many favors; to ask Him to bestow His blessings on all men; and to satisfy His justice for the sins committed against Him.

Jesus says to us, **"As I willingly offer Myself to God the Father for your sins, even so must you willingly offer yourself to Me in the Mass, as a pure and holy victim, together with all your abilities and affections, as wholeheartedly as you can."** Imitation of Christ

*The Bell*

***How should we assist at Mass?***

**We should assist at Mass with reverence, attention, and devotion.**

In the Holy Mass, Jesus Christ offers to God the Father the gift of His Body and Blood, the gift once presented on Calvary. Our part in Holy Mass is to join with Christ in the offering of Himself to God the Father and to receive the Body and Blood of our Lord in Holy Communion.

Because the Mass is the unbloody renewal of the passion and death of Jesus Christ, we should meditate on the sufferings and the love of our Savior while it is being offered.

We may assist at Mass devoutly by following the priest step by step, prayer by prayer, answering the responses and singing the hymns.

Every Sunday, church bells ring out to call the faithful to holy Mass. Devout parents not only answer this call themselves but they see to it that all their children attend Mass, and they begin taking them at an early age, even though the obligation to participate in Mass on Sunday is binding only on children who have reached the use of reason (usually about seven years old).

The practice of assisting at Mass **daily,** instead of just once a week, brings innumerable benefits. Hearing Mass daily can help us to avoid temptation and sin, to find peace amid the trials of life, to grow in the love of God, to thank God for all His blessings, to obtain protection against all dangers, to gain the favors we need, and to shorten the purgatory of our dear, departed ones.

**"To me nothing is so consoling, so piercing, so overcoming, as the Mass—the greatest action that can be on earth."** Cardinal Newman

*The Miraculous Pool* Alinari-Restour

***What is the Sacrament of Penance?***

**Penance is the sacrament by which sins committed after Baptism are forgiven through the absolution of the priest.**

The Gospel tells us that our Lord cured a sick man who had been waiting thirty-eight years for a chance to be the first to descend into the pool near the Sheepgate at Jerusalem. The water of that pool, which miraculously cured a man of whatever infirmity he had, was symbolic of the Sacrament of Penance, by which our souls are healed of the disease of sin.

During His life on earth, Christ forgave sinners by His own authority. Before ascending into heaven, however, in order to provide for our spiritual needs, He conferred that power on His Apostles and their successors.

No man, by his own power and authority, could possibly forgive sins. Only God can do that, because sin is an offense against Him. Saint Thomas declares: "The Church's ministers do not remit sin of their own authority as principal efficient causes. Only God can do that.... They should not be called givers of grace, for that implies authority, but rather ministers of the granting of God's grace."

The priest has the power to forgive sins from Jesus Christ, who said to His Apostles and to their successors in the priesthood: "Receive the Holy Spirit; whose sins you shall forgive, they are forgiven them; and whose sins you shall retain, they are retained" (Jn. 20:22-23).

When we receive the Sacrament of Penance worthily, it restores or increases sanctifying grace in our souls, it remits the eternal punishment, if necessary, and also at least part of the temporal punishment due to our sins; it helps us to avoid sin in the future, and it restores the merits of our good works if they have been lost by mortal sin.

**"If we acknowledge our sins, he is faithful and just to forgive us."**

1 Jn. 1:9

***What must we do to receive the Sacrament of Penance worthily?***

**To receive the Sacrament of Penance worthily, we must: 1) examine our conscience; 2) be sorry for our sins; 3) have the firm purpose of not sinning again; 4) confess our sins to the priest; 5) be willing to perform the penance the priest gives us.**

*The Prodigal Son* Baloni-Alinari

In Christ's parable of the Prodigal Son, the physical suffering of this boy after he left home and squandered his fortune is comparable to the moral suffering of one who strays from God to follow the ways of sin. And the boy's return to his father exemplifies the necessary conditions for a return to God with a good confession.

The Prodigal Son was living in abject poverty when he finally considered the sins he had committed and acknowledged his guilt. We do the same when we **examine our conscience** before confession. With deep sorrow in his heart, he said to himself, "I will go to my father and say to him, 'Father, I have sinned....'" **Sorrow for sins** is so essential to the Sacrament of Penance that God Himself, although omnipotent, cannot forgive the sins of one who is not repentant. The grieving wanderer made up his mind to lead a much different life in the future. A really contrite heart has **the firm purpose of not sinning again.** When he reached home, he humbly confessed his wickedness. St. Ambrose comments: "God knows all things, yet He requires a sincere **confession** of our sins." By his words to his father, "I am no longer worthy to be called your son; make me as one of your hired men," the repentant son showed his willingness to do penance for his evil deeds, as we must be **willing to perform the penance** given us by the priest.

**"Do not lose heart because of the enormity and multitude of your failures: the mercy which God offers and promises to those who repent infinitely surpasses all our excesses."** St. Thomas

*The Lost Drachma* John Millais—From the Gospel Edit. Ist Ital. d'Arti Graf. of Bergamo

***What is an examination of conscience?***

**An examination of conscience is a sincere effort to call to mind all the sins we have committed since our last worthy confession.**

In telling the parable of the Lost Coin, Christ asked, "What woman, having ten drachmas, if she loses one drachma, does not light a lamp and sweep the house and search carefully until she finds it?"

The careful search made by the woman in the parable is an eloquent reminder to us to search our conscience diligently, before going to confession, for sins we may have committed and then forgotten. For we cannot confess and detest our sins if we do not remember them. When recalled, they fill us with grief and the desire to be free of them as quickly as possible.

Before making our examination of conscience, we should ask God's help to know our sins and to confess them with sincere sorrow.

We can make a good examination of conscience by calling to mind the commandments of God and of the Church, and the particular duties of our state in life, and by asking ourselves how we may have sinned with regard to them, by thought, word, deed or omission, since our last worthy confession.

The examination should not be made hastily, but neither with excessive anxiety.

**A humble confession excludes every excuse or pretense. "If you excuse yourselves, God accuses you; if you accuse yourselves, God excuses you."**

St. Augustine

### *What is contrition?*

**Contrition is sincere sorrow for having offended God, and hatred for the sins we have committed, with a firm purpose of sinning no more.**

*The Crusade for the Liberation of the Holy Land* Grandi-Anderson

This stirring scene of a battle in the wars of the Crusades, which were fought in the Middle Ages to free the Holy Land from the power of the infidels, offers a vivid picture of contrition. Amid the confusion and din of battle, the dying soldier in the foreground has no thought for anything but his soul. Reverently he kisses the crucifix, manifesting in this way his love of the Redeemer and his sorrow for his sins.

God will not forgive us any sin unless we are sincerely sorry for it.

It is not enough merely to say that we are sorry for our sins; we must really mean it. We must sincerely detest them and firmly intend not to commit them again. However, we do not have to feel our sorrow, for contrition is an act of the will, not of the feelings.

Contrition is deep sorrow for having offended God, for having merited His punishments, for having stained our soul.

If we are sorry for purely natural reasons, as for example, because we are ashamed of our weakness in falling into sin or because we fear that people will come to know, or for any other similar motive, we do not have true contrition, and cannot be forgiven.

To obtain God's pardon, we must be sorry for **all** our mortal sins.

We should try to have sorrow for all our venial sins, too, and if we have only venial sins to confess, then we must be sorry for at least one of them or for some sin of our past life which we confess.

**"Sincere sorrow for having sinned is an infinitely desirable treasure. It brings inestimable joy to the soul of man, and obtains great energy for the will."**

St. Bernard

*The Crucifixion* Stef. Dell'Arzere-Alinari

***How many kinds of contrition are there?***

**There are two kinds of contrition: perfect contrition and imperfect contrition.**

Sin is the greatest evil because it is an offense against God, the supreme Good.

God, however, is always ready to forgive us, if we turn to Him to ask His pardon, tell Him we are sorry and promise not to sin again.

Our contrition is **perfect** when we are sorry for our sins because they offend God our Father, infinitely good and amiable, and are the cause of the passion and death of our Redeemer, Jesus Christ.

An example of an act of **perfect contrition** is: "O my God, I am sorry for my sins because they offended You, who are all good and deserving of all my love."

A person in mortal sin can regain the state of grace before receiving the Sacrament of Penance by making an act of perfect contrition with the sincere purpose of going to confession.

If we have the misfortune to commit a mortal sin, we should ask God's pardon at once, make an act of perfect contrition, and go to confession as soon as we can. Although it is true that when our sins are forgiven by perfect contrition we may not receive Holy Communion until we have been to confession, yet, in the meantime, we are in the state of grace and able to gain merit.

An excellent way to arouse perfect sorrow for sins is to contemplate Christ on the cross and near Him, His sorrowful Mother.

**"Her sins, many as they are, shall be forgiven her, because she has loved much."** Lk. 7:47

*St. Jerome Meditates on Judgment* Marinus-Anderson

***When is our contrition imperfect?***

**Our contrition is imperfect when we are sorry for our sins because they are hateful in themselves or because we fear God's punishment.**

In the solitude of the desert, where he practiced austere penance, St. Jerome trembled at the thought of death and judgment. So impressed was he by these truths that he could almost hear the trumpets calling all men to render an account of their lives to God.

Indeed, God is just and must punish sin either in this life or in the next, for it offends Him. Rightly, then, do we poor sinners fear the just judgments of God.

**Imperfect contrition,** or **attrition,** as it is sometimes called, is the sorrow of those who repent because they fear the divine punishments, eternal or temporal, which they have merited by their sins, or simply because by sinning they have stained their soul, disfigured it and degraded it.

Their sorrow springs from fear, not love. It is not the sorrow of devoted children, but rather of servants who fear their master.

An act of imperfect contrition cannot obtain forgiveness of mortal sin without the absolution of a priest.

However, to receive the Sacrament of Penance worthily, imperfect contrition is sufficient.

We should always try to have perfect contrition in the Sacrament of Penance because it is more pleasing to God.

**"Confession appeases the wrath of God; it is the remedy for temptations and sins of every kind; it communicates grace, light, strength, and joy."**

Cornelius A' Lapide

*Magdalen at the Feet of Jesus* Moretto da Br.-Alinari

***What is the firm purpose of sinning no more?***

**The firm purpose of sinning no more is the sincere resolve not only to avoid sin but to avoid as far as possible the near occasions of sin.**

When Jesus dined in the home of Simon the Pharisee, a woman who was a sinner came with an alabaster jar of ointment and bathed the Lord's feet with her tears, wiped them with her hair, kissed them, and anointed them with ointment. And Christ, knowing her to be truly sorry for her sins, said to her, "Your sins are forgiven."

This repentant woman, whose sorrow was so great, changed her life and attained great sanctity and was very dear to our Lord.

"O man," says St. Peter Chrysologus, "beware not to despair! If you have sinned, you have but to make reparation to a very merciful Creditor. Do you want forgiveness? Love! Charity covers a multitude of sins."

One who is sincerely sorry for his sins is also resolved not to commit them again. This firm purpose of amendment does not necessarily exclude the fear that a person may repeat his sin in the future. It does mean that, at the time, relying fully upon God's grace, he sincerely intends never to commit this sin again and he is determined to keep away from all mortal sins.

The firm purpose of amendment includes also the intention to remain away from persons, places, or things that may easily lead to sin. For if we do not avoid the occasions of sin, we will end by falling again: "He that loves danger shall perish in it" (Eccl. 3:27).

**"Do not be led astray: 'evil companions corrupt good morals.'"** 1 Cor. 15:33

***What is Confession?***

**Confession is the telling of our sins to an authorized priest for the purpose of obtaining forgiveness.**

Among the most touching of Gospel stories is the story of the conversion of Zacchaeus. This man, a rich publican of Jericho, tried to see Jesus when He passed through that city, but could not, on account of the crowd, for he was small of stature. Therefore he ran on ahead and climbed a sycamore tree. When our Lord drew near, He looked up, saw him and said, "Zacchaeus, make haste and come down; for I must stay in your house today." Zacchaeus hastened down to welcome Jesus with great joy. But the people began to murmur, "He has gone to be the guest of a man who is a sinner." Whereupon Zacchaeus said to Jesus, "Behold, Lord, I give one-half of my possessions to the poor, and if I have defrauded anyone of anything, I restore it fourfold."

*Zacchaeus* W. Hole-From "The Life of Our Lord Jesus Christ" Reason and Faith-Madrid

Jesus replied: "Today salvation has come to this house. The Son of Man came to seek and to save what was lost" (cf. Lk. 19:1-11).

How spontaneous, sincere and humble was that confession of Zacchaeus!

We must confess our sins because Jesus Christ obliges us to do so in these words, spoken to the Apostles and to their successors in the priesthood: **"Whose sins you shall forgive, they are forgiven them; and whose sins you shall retain, they are retained"** (Jn. 20:23).

These words oblige us to confess our sins, because the priest cannot know whether he should forgive or retain our sins unless we tell them to him. We should not let shame prevent us from doing so. The priest will forgive our sins in the name of Christ, advise and encourage us, help us solve our doubts, and guide our future conduct. Never, under any circumstances, not even to save his life, will he reveal our sins to anyone.

**"Human justice only awaits a confession in order to condemn; God, on the contrary, only awaits a confession in order to absolve."** Cornelius A' Lapide

*The Sacraments* Crespi-Anderson

***Is it necessary to confess every sin?***

**It is necessary to confess every mortal sin which has not yet been confessed and forgiven; it is not necessary to confess our venial sins, but it is better to do so.**

To make a good confession, we must confess all the mortal sins we have committed, telling their kind, the number of times we have committed each mortal sin, and any circumstances changing their nature.

We must also confess whether the sin was in thought, word, or deed.

If we cannot remember the exact number of our mortal sins, we should tell the number as nearly as possible, or say how often we have committed the sins in a day, a week, a month, or a year.

If we knowingly conceal a mortal sin in confession the sins we confess are not forgiven; moreover, we commit a mortal sin of sacrilege.

A person who has knowingly concealed a mortal sin in confession must confess that he has made a bad confession, tell the sin he has concealed, mention the sacraments he has received since that time, and confess all the other mortal sins he has committed since his last good confession.

If, instead, without our fault, we forget to confess a mortal sin, we may receive Holy Communion, because we have made a good confession and the sin is forgiven; but we must tell the sin in confession if it again comes to our mind.

We are not obliged to confess venial sins, but it is better to do so, because we have more assurance that they are forgiven and because we receive from the Sacrament of Penance special graces to help us avoid them in the future.

**"Be careful at present and sorry for your sins, that on the day of judgment you may be secure with the blessed."** Imitation of Christ

***Why does the priest give us a penance after confession?***

**The priest gives us a penance after confession that we may make some atonement to God for our sins, receive help to avoid them in the future, and make some satisfaction for the temporal punishment due to them.**

*Christian Charity* D. Schidone-Alinari

The Sacrament of Penance, worthily received, always takes away all eternal punishment; but it does not always take away all temporal punishment.

Temporal punishment is the punishment or penance that we have to suffer for our sins either here on earth or in purgatory. The dispositions with which one receives the Sacrament of Penance determine the amount of temporal punishment which will be taken away.

God requires temporal punishment for sin to satisfy His justice, to teach us the great evil of sin, and to warn us not to sin again.

Christ, by His death on the cross, made more than adequate satisfaction to atone for all the temporal punishment due to all the sins of mankind; but God wants us to perform works of penance ourselves in order to receive all the benefits of the satisfaction of Christ.

Ordinarily, the penance that the priest gives is a few prayers to be recited with devotion and gratitude to God. At times it may be a good deed to perform.

Besides the penance imposed after confession, the chief means of satisfying the debt of our temporal punishment are: prayer, attending Mass, fasting, almsgiving, the patient endurance of sufferings, and indulgences.

We should do as much penance for our sins as we can, in order to pay the debt for our temporal punishment in this life, and not in purgatory.

**"Everyone who sins ought to pay back the honor of which he has robbed God; and this is the satisfaction which every sinner owes to God."**

St. Anselm

*The Paralytic* Tissot-From "The Life of Jesus Christ"

***What is meant by the commandment to confess our sins at least once a year?***

**By the commandment to confess our sins at least once a year is meant that we are strictly obliged to make a good confession within the year, if we have a mortal sin to confess.**

Four men brought a certain poor paralytic to Christ to be cured. Being unable to get through the crowds who had gathered to hear Him preach, they lowered him in a sheet through an opening in the roof. Moved by such faith, the Divine Master said: "Take courage, son. Your sins are forgiven you." At that some of the Scribes said within themselves: "This man blasphemes!" And Jesus, knowing their thoughts, said: "Why do you harbor evil thoughts in your hearts? For which is easier to say, 'Your sins are forgiven you,' or to say, 'Arise and walk'? But that you may know that the Son of Man has power on earth to forgive sins"—then He said to the paralytic—"Arise, take up your pallet and go to your house." And he arose, and went away to his house (cf. Mt. 9:1-8).

Christ offers us the opportunity to have our sins forgiven in the Sacrament of Penance. In better days for the Church, it was not necessary to oblige people to go to confession; whoever fell into sin hastened to confess himself. With the passing of the years, however, Christians lost their horror of sin, and remained for long periods of time in that miserable state. For this reason, the Church commanded the faithful to go to confession at least once a year.

There is no particular time in which the yearly confession must be made. However, owing to the obligation to receive Holy Communion at Easter time, it is customary to discharge the duty of annual confession at the same time.

Although the requirement is only once a year, we should go to confession often because frequent confession helps us to overcome temptation, to keep in the state of grace, and to grow in virtue.

**"If we say that we have no sin, we deceive ourselves."** 1 Jn. 1:8

*The Portiuncula Indulgence Granted to St. Francis* Murillo-Anderson

***What is an indulgence?***

**An indulgence is the remission granted by the Church of the temporal punishment due to the sins already forgiven.**

One night our Lord and His Blessed Mother appeared to St. Francis of Assisi in the little church of the Portiuncula and told him to make any request he wished. The saint asked and obtained that a plenary indulgence be granted to all those who, being sorry for their sins, should visit that church.

An indulgence does not take away sin. By an indulgence the Church merely wipes out or lessens the temporal punishment due to sins already forgiven, applying to us from her **spiritual treasury** part of the infinite satisfaction of Jesus Christ and of the superabundant satisfaction of the Blessed Virgin Mary and the saints.

God accepts the satisfaction of His divine Son and of the saints for the benefit of other members of the Church.

To gain indulgences, we must be in the state of grace, have at least a general intention of gaining them and perform the works required by the Church.

A **plenary** indulgence is the remission of all the temporal punishment due to our sins. A **partial** indulgence is the remission of only part of it.

There are numerous indulgences that we may gain for ourselves and for the souls in purgatory. Wise is he who gains as many as possible.

**"And I will give you the keys of the kingdom of heaven; and whatever you shall bind on earth shall be bound in heaven, and whatever you shall loose on earth shall be loosed in heaven."** Mt. 16:19-20

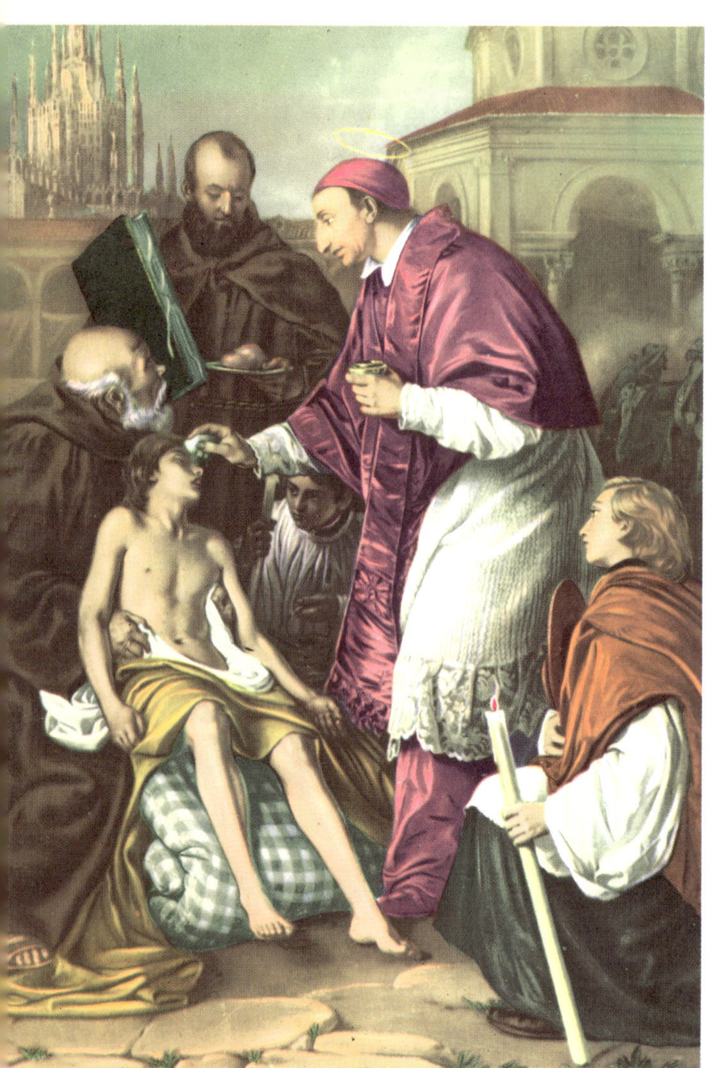

*St. Charles Borromeo* Marcinelli-Anderson

***What is Anointing of the Sick?***

**Anointing of the Sick is the sacrament which, through the anointing with blessed oil by the priest, and through his prayer, gives health and strength to the soul and sometimes to the body when we are in danger of death from sickness, accident, or old age.**

During the terrible plague which raged in Milan in the year 1576, St. Charles Borromeo, Archbishop of Milan, performed wonderful deeds of charity on behalf of his stricken people. He dedicated himself entirely to their service. In the illustration, he is shown administering Anointing of the Sick to a dying youth.

Jesus Christ instituted the Sacrament of the Anointing of the Sick for the spiritual consolation of Christians who are seriously ill.

This sacrament increases sanctifying grace and prepares the soul for entrance into heaven by removing venial sins and the remains of sin. It even takes away mortal sin when the sick person is unconscious or otherwise unaware that he is not properly disposed, but has made an act of imperfect contrition. It gives the strength to suffer patiently and to resist temptation. It even restores or improves the health of the body when this is good for the soul.

Anointing of the Sick should be received as soon as there is danger of death. In fact, it is advisable to call the priest to visit the sick in any serious illness, even though there be no apparent danger of death, as it is the duty of the priest to visit the sick and to administer to them the sacraments they need.

In case of sudden or unexpected death a priest should be called always, because absolution and Anointing of the Sick can be given conditionally for some time after apparent death.

**"My son, in your sickness, neglect not yourself, but pray to the Lord, and he shall heal you."** Eccl. 38:9

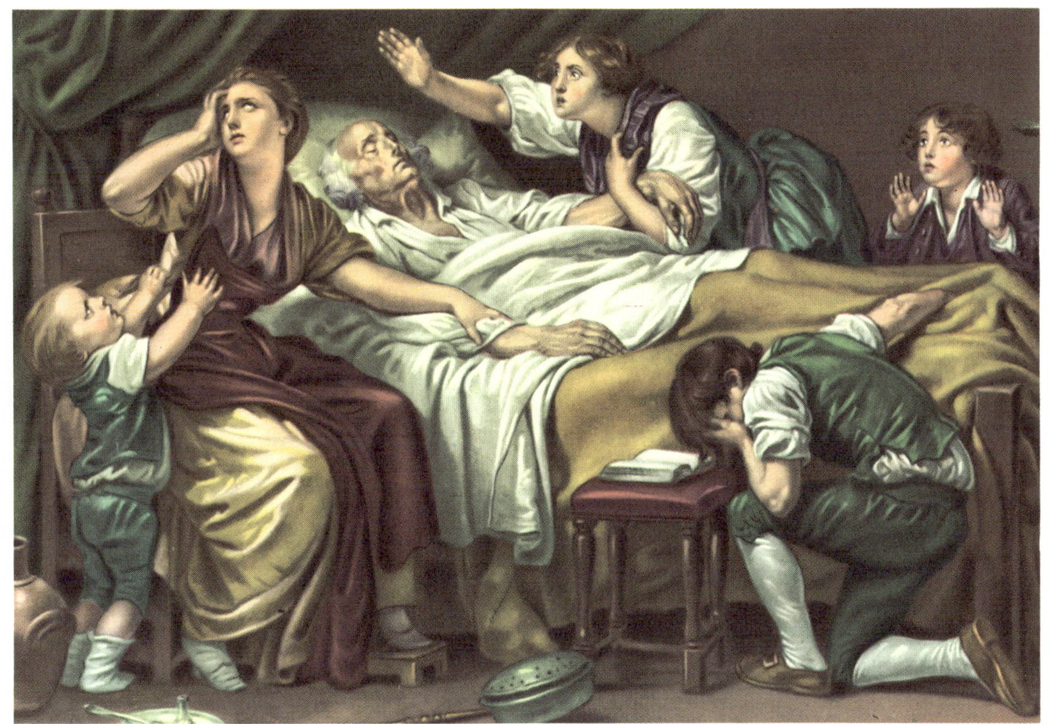

*Death* Crenze-Anderson

***Who should receive Anointing of the Sick?***

**All Catholics who have reached the use of reason and are in danger of death from sickness, accident, or old age should receive Anointing of the Sick.**

When shall we die? How? Where? Will we die at the end of a long life or in our youth? from a lingering disease or in an accident? at home or on the street? We can answer none of these questions. We can only know for certain that death will come to us as it comes to all men. Nothing is more certain than death, nothing more uncertain than its hour. And upon the state of our soul at that last hour depends our eternal destiny.

The face of the dying father in the illustration is serene and peaceful. In general, we die as we have lived.

It is a great act of charity toward a person in danger of death to call a priest for him, for soon he may have to face God, his just Judge. We should pray for and with the sick person and do all we can to help him prepare himself well for the reception of the last sacraments.

There is no hour in life when a man has greater need of God's merciful help and strengthening grace than the hour when he must ready himself to leave everything behind and cross the threshold into eternity.

**"Send heavenward your daily prayers, that after death your spirit may be worthy to pass happily to our Lord."** Imitation of Christ

*The Ordination of St. Lawrence* Fracassini-Anderson

***What is Holy Orders?***

**Holy Orders is the sacrament through which men receive the power and grace to perform the sacred duties of bishops, priests or deacons.**

Christ chose the twelve Apostles from among His disciples and in a special way deputed and consecrated them for the exercise of spiritual ministrations. And they, who could not mistake the will of Christ, consecrated bishops and ordained priests and deacons.

Our Lord instituted the priesthood at the Last Supper when, after consecrating the bread and wine, He said, "Do this in remembrance of me" (Lk. 22:19).

The Sacrament of Holy Orders imprints on the soul a character, lasting forever, which is a special sharing in the priesthood of Christ, and which gives the priest special supernatural powers, chief among which are the power to change bread and wine into the Body and Blood of Christ in the holy Sacrifice of the Mass and the power to forgive sins in the Sacrament of Penance.

We owe reverence and honor to the priest because he is the representative of Christ Himself and the dispenser of His mysteries: "Let a man so account us, as servants of Christ and stewards of the mysteries of God" (1 Cor. 4:1).

**It is a very great privilege to be a priest. Indeed, one enters the priesthood to sanctify his soul and to labor faithfully for the extension of Christ's kingdom.**

*The Virgin's Espousal* Raphael-Alinari

***What is the Sacrament of Matrimony?***

**Matrimony is the sacrament by which a baptized man and a baptized woman bind themselves for life in a lawful marriage and receive the graces needed to be faithful for life, and to discharge their duties.**

This painting by Raphael depicts the espousal of the Blessed Virgin Mary to St. Joseph, who was to be the protector of her virginity and the foster-father of her divine Son. How blessed was the union of these two privileged creatures!

God instituted marriage when He made Eve as a helpmate for Adam in the Garden of Eden. In the New Testament Jesus Christ raised every true marriage between a baptized man and a baptized woman to the dignity of a sacrament.

For the good of husband and wife, for the physical and spiritual welfare of their children, and for the good of society, God has decreed that the marriage bond last until the death of husband or wife: "What therefore God has joined together, let no man put asunder" (Mt. 19:6). Laws which permit remarriage during the life of husband or wife are contrary to God's laws, and such a marriage is not really a marriage at all, but rather an adulterous union.

The primary end of marriage is the procreation and education of offspring.

St. Thomas declares: "Marriage has three blessings. The first is children, to be received and raised for God's service. The second is the loyal faith whereby each serves the other. The third is the sacrament, which signifies the inseparable union of Christ with His Church."

**"Wives, be subject to your husbands as is becoming in the Lord. Husbands, love your wives and do not be bitter towards them."**

Col. 3:18-19

*The Wedding of Emperor Frederick I* Tiepolo-Anderson

***What is the ordinary law of the Church to be observed at the wedding of a Catholic?***

**The ordinary law of the Church to be observed at the wedding of a Catholic is this: a Catholic can contract a true marriage only in the presence of an authorized priest or deacon and two witnesses.**

In this painting, Tiepolo has captured all the pomp and color which attended the wedding of the Emperor Frederick I, called Frederick Barbarossa.

The Catholic Church alone has the right to make laws regulating the marriages of baptized persons because Matrimony is a sacrament, and the Church alone has authority over the sacraments. The state has the authority to make laws concerning the merely civil effects of these marriages, that is, the rights and obligations of husband and wife as citizens.

According to Church law, two Catholics can be validly married only in the presence of an authorized priest or deacon and two witnesses. This canonical form is also to be used for contracting mixed marriages. If, however, serious difficulties stand in the way of observing the canonical form, local ordinaries have the right to dispense from the canonical form in any mixed marriage. But the bishops' conference is to determine norms according to which the said dispensation may be granted.

A man and woman planning to marry should be well aware of the rights and obligations of the married state and should be of a proper age to assume its responsibilities.

**"Marriage was instituted for the one purpose of procreating children, so that they might be born properly and decently."** St. Augustine

*St. Cecilia and Valerian* Domenichino-Alinari

***What is necessary to receive Matrimony worthily?***

**To receive the Sacrament of Matrimony worthily it is necessary to be in the state of grace, to know the duties of married life, and to obey the marriage laws of the Church.**

St. Cecilia was a noble Roman maiden who, when constrained by her guardian to marry the pagan, Valerian, spoke so well of her religion, of the holiness of our body, which is watched over and protected by an angel, that her husband was completely won over to veneration for her and even asked to be baptized.

A happy marriage is prepared for by praying that God may direct the choice, by seeking the advice of parents and confessors, by practicing the virtues, especially chastity, and by frequently receiving the sacraments.

Those couples have the best hope of a harmonious married life who are of the same religion, and of like character, who nourish a tender affection for each other and are ready to share alike both the joys and burdens of their state.

In the Sacrament of Matrimony God gives the Christian husband and wife special graces to love each other faithfully, to bear with each other's faults, and to bring up their children properly.

Whoever receives Matrimony in mortal sin marries validly, but commits a grave sin of sacrilege; moreover, the graces he was to have received are suspended until he makes a good confession.

The best way to obtain an abundance of God's blessings upon one's marriage is by being married at a Nuptial Mass and by receiving Holy Communion.

**"House and riches are given by parents; but a prudent wife is properly from the Lord."** Prv. 19:14

*Prayer* Schnorr

***What is prayer?***

**Prayer is the lifting up of our minds and hearts to God.**

In Schnorr's expressive painting, the angels on high are praising the Lord, while the great King David in the center is singing hymns of joy to the music of his harp before the Ark of the Covenant. On the left is Hannah thanking God for having given her a son, and to the right, also singing hymns of praise, are the three men who were miraculously preserved from harm when thrown into a furnace for refusing to adore false gods.

It is the high privilege of angels and men to speak with God in prayer.

It is a very easy thing to pray. In fact, a prayer may be both brief and efficacious. The Gospel gives us many examples of short, simple prayers: The blind man's plea, "Lord, that I may see"; the prayer of the publican, "Lord, be merciful to me, a sinner"; the cry of the Apostles during the storm on the lake, "Lord, save us! We are perishing"; the centurion's petition, "Lord, only say the word, and my servant will be healed"; the appeal of the Good Thief on the cross, "Lord, remember me when you come into your kingdom." All these prayers were answered immediately.

We may pray anywhere, anytime, for God is always present and always disposed to hear us and come to our aid. But the best place to pray is in church, the house of God.

Particularly pleasing to God is prayer in common: "Where two or three are gathered together for my sake," said our Lord, "there am I in the midst of them" (Mt. 18:20). How much God blesses the family that prays together!

**"Pray with your attention fixed on the words and pray from the heart."** St. Francis de Sales

***What is meditation, or mental prayer?***

**Meditation, or mental prayer, is that prayer by which we unite our heart with God while thinking of His holy truths.**

*Meditation* Dom. Feli-Alinari

We can pray with our soul alone or with both our body and soul; thus we have two types of prayer: **mental** prayer and **vocal** prayer.

The young woman in the illustration is contemplating a skull and considering what awaits everyone at the end of life: death, judgment and heaven or hell. This is meditation.

Ten minutes of meditation each day on such subjects as the eternal truths, and especially the life and passion of our Lord, is a great help to continual spiritual progress. It is best made in the morning when it strengthens us for the cares of the day and disposes us to do God's will in all things.

Should you like, for your spiritual profit, to become acquainted with mental prayer, or meditation, then follow these simple steps: place yourself in the presence of God and implore His assistance; read some spiritual book with attention or represent to your mind the mystery on which you desire to meditate, and then make reflections and considerations until your affections are moved and raised up to God; add a practical resolution to correct your faults; return thanks to God for His goodness and mercy, and implore Him and our Lady to bless your resolution, that you may faithfully put it into practice.

Many go astray in life because they neglect to consider the great affair of their eternal salvation and what they must do in order to be saved. Those, instead, who habitually reflect on these things lead good lives, for meditation and mortal sin cannot exist together.

**"Our main concern in prayer must be to speak to God and to hear God speak in the depths of our heart."** St. Francis de Sales

*Daniel in the Lions' Den* Dorè-Garzanti

***What is vocal prayer?***

**Vocal prayer is that prayer which comes from the mind and heart and is spoken by the lips.**

The prophet Daniel, who was a royal official of King Darius the Mede, was accused of violating the law of the empire which forbade prayers addressed to anyone but the king. The command notwithstanding, Daniel had prayed to the one true God, prostrating himself on the ground with his face turned towards Jerusalem.

For his fidelity to his God, Daniel was thrown into a den of lions. But he cried out to the Lord confidently and was not even touched by the famished beasts. Coming out of the den safe and sound on the following day, he declared to the king: "My God has shut up the mouths of the lions, and they have not hurt me."

How marvelous are the effects of prayer!

Vocal prayer must never become a mere mechanical recitation of well-known prayers. It is not true prayer unless it comes from the mind and from a devout heart. Distractions in our prayers, however, are not displeasing to God, unless they are willful.

We may be sure that God always hears our prayers if we pray properly because our Lord has promised: "If you ask the Father anything in my name, he will give it to you" (Jn. 16:23).

Prayer is the condition God has laid down for us to obtain His graces and blessings. He always answers our prayers in the way that is best for us.

Through prayer we can obtain from our loving Father in heaven the grace to resist temptations, to grow in His love, to persevere in leading a good life, and most important of all, the grace of our eternal salvation.

**"He who prays will be saved; he who does not pray will be lost."**

St. Alphonsus de Liguori

*The Prayer of the Pharisee and Publican* Schnorr

***How should we pray?***

**We should pray: 1) with attention; 2) with a conviction of our own helplessness and our dependence upon God; 3) with a great desire for the graces we beg of Him; 4) with loving trust in His goodness; 5) with perseverance.**

To teach us how to pray, Jesus told this parable: "Two men went up to the temple to pray, the one a Pharisee and the other a publican. The Pharisee stood and began to pray thus within himself: 'O God, I thank you that I am not like the rest of men, robbers, dishonest, adulterers, or even like this publican. I fast twice a week; I pay tithes on all that I possess.' But the publican, standing afar off, would not so much as lift up his eyes to heaven, but kept striking his breast, saying, 'O God, be merciful to me a sinner.'

"I tell you, this man went back to his home justified rather than the other; for everyone who exalts himself shall be humbled, and he who humbles himself shall be exalted" (Lk. 18:10-15).

Prayer is conversation with God. Hence we must try to make our prayer pleasing to the God of infinite majesty and divine mercy. We should pray with humility, perseverance, resignation to the divine will, and confidence in Christ's promise: "All things whatever you ask for in prayer, believe that you shall receive, and they shall come to you" (Mk. 11:24).

Let us never lose heart, for no prayer is offered in vain: "Everyone who asks, receives" (Mt. 7:8).

**"When we pray, beloved brethren, we ought to be watchful and earnest with our whole heart, intent on our prayers. All worldly thoughts should be banished, and our soul should think of nothing but the object of its prayer."**

St. Cyprian

*The Prayer of Moses* Schnorr

***Why do we pray?***

**We pray: 1) to adore God, expressing to Him our love and loyalty; 2) to thank Him for His favors; 3) to obtain from Him the pardon of our sins and the remission of their punishment; 4) to ask for graces and blessings for ourselves and others.**

The chosen people of God overcame their numerous enemies with prayer and trust in God more than with arms. On one occasion, a very powerful enemy fell upon them in the desert. Moses sent his army to battle them, and he ascended a mountain to pray. As long as he held his arms outstretched toward heaven, Israel overcame; but when he let his arms fall from fatigue, the enemy overcame. Therefore, Aaron and Hur seated him upon a rock and held up his arms until the Israelites put their enemy to flight.

Prayer is a debt we owe to God: a debt of adoration, because He is our Lord and Master; a debt of thanksgiving, because He is our first and greatest Benefactor; a debt of sorrow, because we have offended Him by our sins.

Prayer is a duty because Jesus Christ commanded us to pray and because, in general, spiritual and temporal graces are granted only to those who pray.

So immense is the goodness of God that He has a greater desire to give than we have to receive, and when we pray, He grants much more than what we request.

**"You shall pray to me, and I will hear you. You shall find me, when you shall seek me with all your heart."** Jer. 29:12-13

*Our Father*

Aubert—From the Gospel
Edit. by Instituto d'Arti Graf. of Bergamo

***Why is the "Our Father" the best of all prayers?***

**The "Our Father" is the best of all prayers because it is the Lord's Prayer, taught us by Jesus Christ Himself, and because it is a prayer of perfect and unselfish love.**

The "Our Father" is the most perfect, the most sublime, the most holy, and the most useful of all prayers, primarily because it was composed by God, but also because in saying it we offer ourselves entirely to God and ask from Him the best things, not only for ourselves, but also for our neighbor.

Contemplate the picture of Jesus teaching His disciples this divine prayer. What an example of devotion!

In the Lord's Prayer, we address God by the sweet name of "Father" and we ask first of all for that which pertains to His glory: that He be known and honored everywhere; that the kingdom of His grace may be spread throughout the world; and that He may be obeyed by all men.

In the other four petitions of the prayer, we ask God to grant us spiritual and temporal graces. We ask Him: to give us every day all that we need for our soul and our body; to forgive us our sins, as we forgive those who offend us; to give us the grace to overcome temptations; and to protect us from all harm, especially from harm to our souls.

Happy the man who says this admirable prayer frequently and fervently!

**"What will He not give to us—who made us His own children?"**

St. Augustine

# CORPORAL WORKS OF MERCY

***What is the first corporal work of mercy?***

**The first corporal work of mercy is to feed the hungry.**

The noble matron giving food to the poor is St. Frances of Rome. Her doorway was always crowded with the hungry, and to them she gave everything she did not absolutely need. What a marvelous example of charity!

Our charity towards our neighbor must be an active charity; we cannot be content with beautiful words only, but must do good to others. "All that you wish men to do to you, even so do you also to them" (Mt. 7:12).

The **corporal works of mercy** are those which relieve our neighbor in his material need.

"To feed the hungry" is the first corporal work of mercy. Perhaps we have never known the terrible misfortune of being unable to appease our hunger, but there are many needy in the world.

We all are obliged, according to our condition in life, and according to the need of our neighbor, to do good to others, first to our own relatives, to those of our own faith, and to our friends, giving aid and comfort. "Let us do good to all men," says St. Paul, "but especially to those who are of the household of faith" (Gal. 6:10).

Giving alms to the missions, helping to support orphan asylums, and the charitable institutions of the Church are practical ways of performing works of mercy.

In doing good to our neighbor, however, we should not be moved by natural motives, as, for example, to win praise or to be rewarded on this earth. Rather, our sole motive should be the love of God.

**"When you give alms, do not let your left hand know what your right hand is doing, so that your alms may be given in secret; and your Father, who sees in secret, will reward you."**

Mt. 6:3-4

*St. Frances of Rome* Martinelli-Alinari

***What is the second corporal work of mercy?***

**The second corporal work of mercy is to give drink to the thirsty.**

*Charity* Mussini-Brogi

At the last judgment, we will be asked to give an account of how we treated our neighbor during our lifetime. If we were charitable, our Lord will extend to us the sweet invitation: "Come, blessed of my Father, take possession of the kingdom prepared for you from the foundation of the world; for I was hungry and you gave me to eat; I was thirsty and you gave me to drink; I was a stranger and you took me in; naked and you covered me; sick and you visited me; I was in prison and you came to me."

Then the just will ask Him, "Lord, when did we see you hungry, and feed you; thirsty, and give you drink? And when did we see you a stranger, and take you in; or naked, and clothe you? Or when did we see you sick, or in prison, and come to you?

And in answer, Christ will say to them, "Amen I say to you, as long as you did it to one of these my least brethren, you did it to me" (cf. Mt. 25:34-41).

No precept of the Gospel is urged more strongly than our duty to practice charity toward one another in every way. Not even the simple act of quenching another's thirst with plain water is overlooked by our Lord: "Whoever gives to one of these little ones but a cup of cold water to drink because he is a disciple, amen I say to you, he shall not lose his reward" (Mt. 10:42).

**"Charity is the pure gold which makes us rich in eternal wealth."**

J. P. Camus

*St. Catherine Gives Clothes to Jesus* Franchi-Alinari

***What is the third corporal work of mercy?***

**The third corporal work of mercy is to clothe the naked.**

St. Catherine of Siena never refused anything to the poor, who begged her charity in the name of Jesus Christ, her heavenly Spouse.

On one occasion, a scantily-clothed beggar asked her for a warm robe and she, without hesitating, handed him her own woolen cloak. He then begged her for an undergarment and the saint gave him one of her father's.

That night, while she was praying, Christ appeared to her under the form of the beggar. In His hand was the cloak she had given away, but it was now adorned with pearls and gems.

"Today you gave me this robe," He said. "Now I give you an invisible one in which to clothe both your soul and your body."

And He Himself attired her in that radiant garment.

From that day on Catherine never suffered the cold again. In fact, through the most severe winters, she would wear light summer clothes.

We, too, must clothe the destitute and suffering members of Christ's Mystical Body. In reward for our generosity, our divine Lord will bestow on us the resplendent robe of His grace.

The Lord tells us: "When you shall see one naked, cover him, and despise not your own flesh" (Is. 58:7).

**"He who has the goods of this world and sees his brother in need and closes his heart to him, how does the love of God abide in him? My dear children, let us not love in word, neither with the tongue, but in deed and in truth."**

1 Jn. 3:17-18

***What is the fourth corporal work of mercy?***

**The fourth corporal work of mercy is to visit the imprisoned.**

St. Vincent de Paul was a tireless apostle of charity. No form of human misery escaped his attention. In his position as head chaplain of French prisons, he often visited and consoled the wretched convicts condemned to hard labor.

On one of his visits, a certain man who had been condemned unjustly expressed his utter despair. He even refused to listen to the saint's exhortations. Then it was that Vincent, in an act of heroic charity, offered to take his place. He had the unfortunate man freed and himself fettered with the prisoner's heavy chain. Thus did he imitate our divine Savior, who sacrificed Himself for all men.

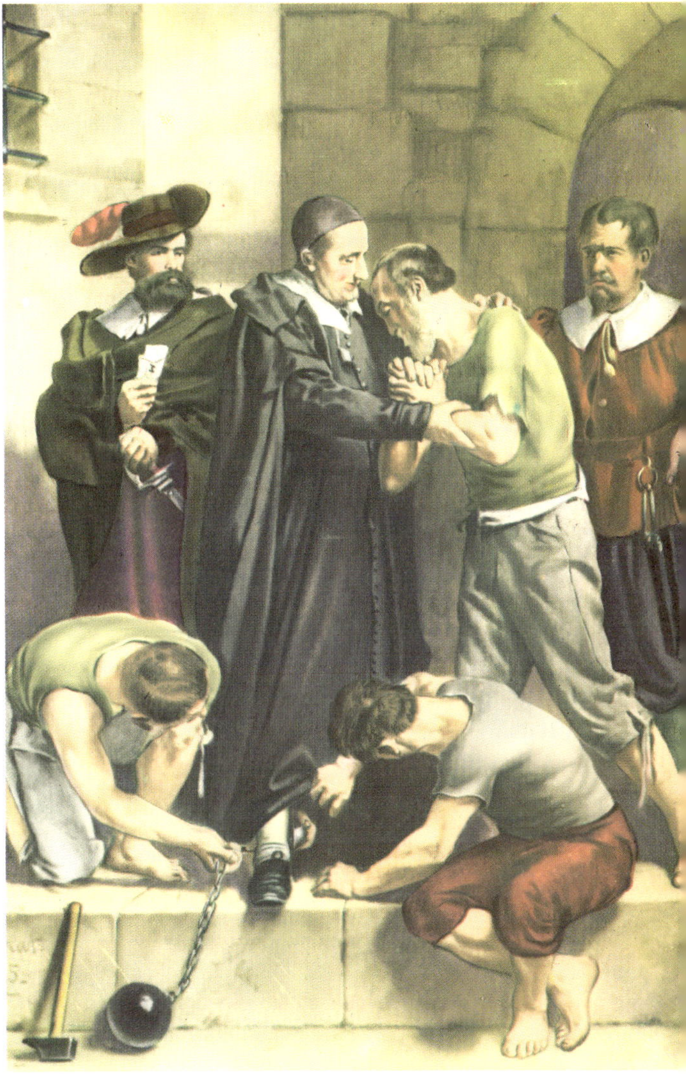

*St. Vincent Visits the Prisoners* Bonnat

Such is the charity of the saints!

In past centuries, entire religious orders of the Church heroically dedicated themselves to the ransoming of prisoners of war who had been made slaves, and of providing them with every kind of spiritual and material help. What great advantages for Christian civilization were wrought by that work of charity!

Prisoners need comfort, encouragement, and good counsel if they are to return to the right path. Those who visit them perform a great act of charity.

**"I was in prison," Jesus will say to His chosen ones, "and you came to me."** Mt. 25:36

*St. Julian's Hospitality* Allori-Anderson

***What is the fifth corporal work of mercy?***

**The fifth corporal work of mercy is to shelter the homeless.**

From the earliest times of the Church, hospitality has been highly regarded among Christians. The traveler has always been welcome and served as though he were Jesus Christ Himself.

The picture illustrates the active charity of St. Julian who, together with his holy wife, dedicated his life to alleviating the discomforts of poor wayfarers. He made his home available to them and welcomed each traveler warmly.

The eminently humane and hospitable work of the monks of the great St. Bernard is a well-known example of the fifth corporal work of mercy. With their famous dogs, these men of God rescue lost travelers in the Alps, braving blizzards and risking their lives to bring them to the shelter of their monastery. It is the charity of Christ which moves them to such heroism.

Unfortunately, however, there are in this world selfish souls who are so engrossed in seeking their own ends that they give no thought to the needs of others; compassion is unknown to them. Over such people the divine Judge will pronounce the dread sentence: "Depart from me, accursed ones, into the everlasting fire which was prepared for the devil and his angels. For...**I was a stranger, and you did not take me in....** Amen I say to you, as long as you did not do it for one of these least ones, you did not do it for me" (Mt. 25:41-45).

In our times, one way of "sheltering the homeless," possible to many, is to provide homes for the poor at low rents.

**"Do not forget to entertain strangers; for thereby some have entertained angels unawares."** Heb. 13:2

***What is the sixth corporal work of mercy?***

**The sixth corporal work of mercy is to visit the sick.**

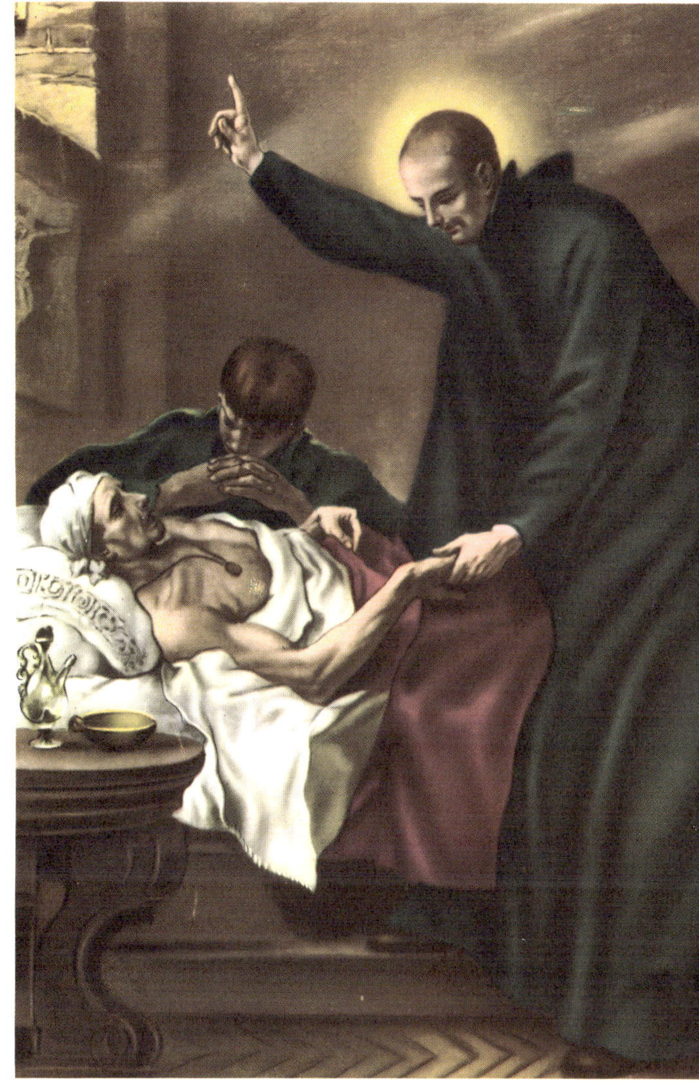

*St. Cajetan Comforts a Dying Man* Ricci-Alinari

St. Cajetan Thiene abandoned a brilliant career in his youth to give himself wholly to the service of God in the care of the sick. As he nursed the sufferers and medicated their wounds, he would speak eloquently of the eternal joys of heaven, and by so doing uplifted their spirits, lessened their anxieties, and consoled their hearts.

The sick have great need of comfort. Tortured by pain, they easily become depressed and disconsolate.

A friendly visit and a kind word can do much to restore serenity to the suffering and to renew their courage. At times, too, their afflictions are increased by an uneasy conscience. If we know that a sick person is resisting God's grace, we must try to convince him, by loving exhortations, to trust in God and to attend to his eternal salvation.

How many times it has happened that a few words, spoken during a visit, were so full of the spirit of charity that they brought back to God a seemingly lost soul, and effected a marvelous conversion at the point of death.

Of all Christians, the sick are the most dear to the maternal heart of the Church. In every age this loving mother has provided for them by building hospitals and raising up entire religious families devoted to their care.

Let us always remember the warning of the Holy Spirit:

**"Be not slow to visit the sick; for by these things you shall be confirmed in love."**

Eccl. 7:39

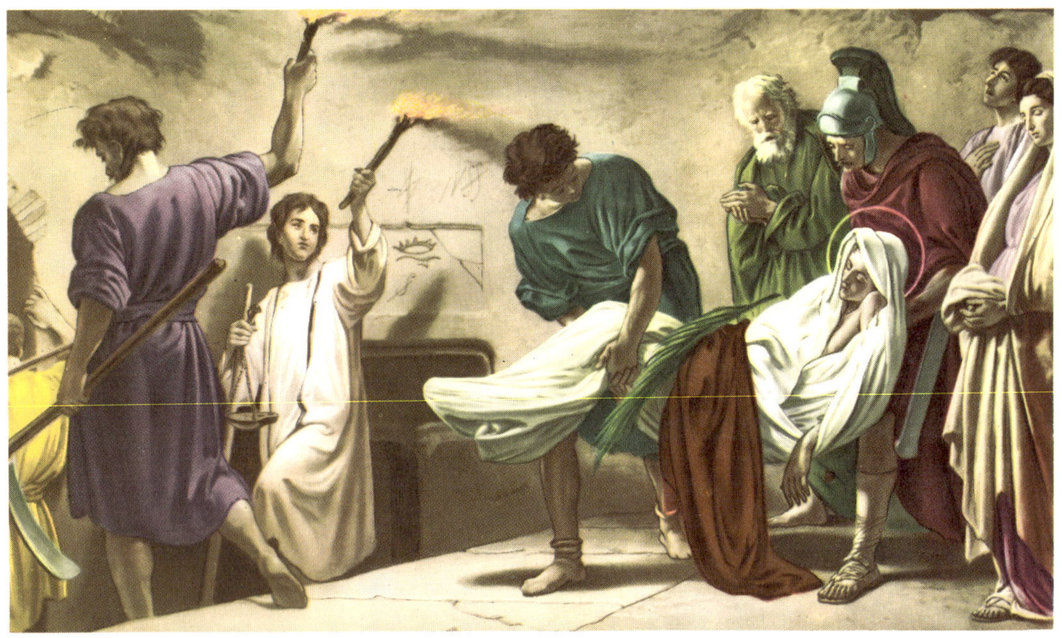

*St. Lawrence Is Carried to the Sepulcher* Grandi-Anderson

***What is the seventh corporal work of mercy?***

**The seventh corporal work of mercy is to bury the dead.**

The Church has always shown veneration for the bodies of her faithful departed, which are sanctified in life by the sacraments and destined to rise one day. For this reason, cemeteries where the remains of the dead rest are blessed. In the early centuries of persecution, they were underground, and were called **catacombs.** The first Christians had great veneration for the bodies of martyrs in particular. In this painting, we note with what reverence the body of the martyr St. Lawrence is being carried through the dark passages to the sacred resting place.

What about cremation? Cremation is not wrong in itself, nor expressly forbidden by the divine law and so it may be allowed by ecclesiastical authority. Christians have always buried their dead for two reasons: 1. our faith in the resurrection of the body, and 2. respect for the body as a member of Christ, a temple of the Holy Spirit.

Of course, cremation can in no way hinder our bodily resurrection, nor is it intrinsically a sign of disrespect for the body. Nonetheless, Christian instinct has always preferred burial.

Church legislation has liberalized considerably rules about cremation. Catholics may now choose to be cremated, unless they do so for reasons hostile to the Christian life, such as a desire to deny the sacredness of the body or the promise of resurrection.

Permission need not be requested any longer, and funeral rites may be carried out at the crematorium.

Despite this new freedom, it should be noted that the Church still prefers the custom of burial in imitation of the Lord. Further, we should discourage the practice of scattering the ashes over open water or the countryside.

It is exquisite charity to accompany the remains of our beloved deceased to the cemetery and to give consolation and aid to his relatives.

**"My son, shed tears over the dead, and neglect not his burial."**

Eccl. 38:16

# SPIRITUAL WORKS OF MERCY

***What is the first spiritual work of mercy?***

**The first spiritual work of mercy is to admonish the sinner.**

The holy Gospel narrates that the Scribes and Pharisees brought to Jesus a woman who had sinned grievously and, setting her in their midst, said to Him, "Master, this woman has just now been caught in adultery. And in the law, Moses commanded us to stone such persons. What do you say?"

Jesus, stooping down, began to write with His finger on the ground. But when they continued asking Him, He raised Himself and said to them: "Let him who is without sin among you be the first to cast a stone at her."

Hearing this, they went away, one by one, beginning with the eldest. Then Jesus said to the woman, "Woman, where are they? Has no one condemned you?" She replied, "No one, Lord." And Jesus said to her: "Neither will I condemn you. Go your way and from now on sin no more" (cf. Jn. 8:3-12).

With what divine sweetness Christ touches and converts the hearts of men!

The **spiritual works of mercy** are those which relieve the spiritual needs of our neighbor.

"To admonish the sinner" is the first spiritual work of mercy.

By **admonishing** is meant correcting another with understanding and charity, at the right time and place, for his own good.

How often a well-chosen word, prompted by the grace of God, is the means of saving someone from sin! We are all obliged, when it is prudent, to admonish sinners and to try to persuade them to turn from evil and to practice virtue. Persons in authority, as for example, parents and teachers, have an even greater obligation than others in this regard.

Sinners may be admonished not only by kind words but also by good example.

**"I desire mercy. I have come to call sinners."**

Mt. 9:13

*Christ and the Adulterous Woman* Allori-Brogi

*Christian Schools* Mariani

***What is the second spiritual work of mercy?***

**The second spiritual work of mercy is to instruct the ignorant.**

The human soul thirsts for truth, above all, for religious truth, which is the highest and most necessary for man, since it teaches him the way of salvation.

The treasures of a great faith tend to diffuse themselves. One speaks of and propagates that which fills his heart: "For out of the abundance of the heart the mouth speaks" (Mt. 12:34).

Those who instruct others in matters of faith—parents, preachers, teachers, missionaries, catechists, and writers—perform a sublime and highly meritorious mission, the very mission of our divine Lord Himself.

In our day, the modern media of communication: press, radio, TV, and motion pictures, offer unlimited opportunities to spread the teachings of Christ to millions of souls. The Church's apostolate in these fields, therefore, deserves our generous support and willing cooperation. For, as true followers of Christ, each one of us must do what he can to share his holy Faith with his neighbor.

To impart knowledge useful in earning a living is another work pleasing to God, if done for His love, because young people must be prepared to make their way in life.

A great example of a Christian educator is St. Jean Baptiste de la Salle, who founded many free schools for the children of the people. Through the efforts of his religious sons, thousands of young people in our day, too, are being given a Christian education.

**"They that instruct many to justice shall shine as stars for all eternity."** Dn. 12:3

***What is the third spiritual work of mercy?***

**The third spiritual work of mercy is to counsel the doubtful.**

As Jesus was going forth on his journey, a certain man running up fell upon his knees before Him, and asked Him, "Good Master, what shall I do to gain eternal life?" And Jesus said to him, "You know the commandments: You shall not commit adultery. You shall not kill. You shall not steal. You shall not bear false witness. You shall not defraud. Honor your father and mother." And he answered and said, "Master, all these things I have kept ever since I was a child." And Jesus, looking upon him, loved him, and said to him, "One thing is wanting to you: go, sell whatever you have, and give to the poor, and you shall have treasure in heaven; and come, follow me" (Mk. 10:21).

*Jesus and the Rich Young Man* Conti

What holy advice Jesus gave that young man!

Doubt is uncertainty about a decision to be made, and since "to err is human," especially if one relies only on his own judgment and rejects the advice of the wise and virtuous, it is clear that giving opportune and prudent counsel is an exquisite form of charity.

Whenever their words are likely to be heeded, Christians must be ready to give helpful advice to those who need it. A word of advice, given after due reflection and prayer, often frees another from agonizing indecision and torment of soul, and prevents a lapse into indifference or a rash, impulsive move.

**"Consult a wise and conscientious man; and seek rather to be instructed by one who is better, than to follow your own inventions."** Imitation of Christ

*L'Innominato and Cardinal Borromeo* Alessandro

***What is the fourth spiritual work of mercy?***

**The fourth spiritual work of mercy is to comfort the sorrowful.**

In Manzoni's immortal novel, "The Betrothed," the characters of Innominato and Frederick Cardinal Borromeo are particularly striking. After a life of untold wickedness, Innominato was touched by God's grace and found in the saintly archbishop a friend and consoler who welcomed him tenderly and helped him obtain forgiveness and peace.

The description of their first meeting is very moving. Turning away from the Cardinal's fatherly embrace, Innominato exclaimed: "God is truly great! God is truly good! I see myself clearly now, I know what I am; all my crimes are before my eyes. I am afraid of myself. And yet I feel a relief and a joy which I have never known in my whole horrible life!" (chapter 23)

The sorrowful are they who are weighed down by grief over some affliction, spiritual or temporal. If we have the spirit of our compassionate Savior, we cannot turn away from a grieving neighbor without showing him sincere sympathy and offering him whatever consolation we can.

They who forget themselves and their own troubles to comfort their afflicted neighbor, inspiring him bravely to bear the cross of our Lord, to think of the happiness that awaits us in heaven, to hope in God, and to be resigned to His divine will, endear themselves to the heart of Christ, who will, in turn, be their comfort and joy.

**"Be not wanting in comforting them that weep, and walk with them that mourn."** Eccl. 7:38

***What is the fifth spiritual work of mercy?***

**The fifth spiritual work of mercy is to bear wrongs patiently.**

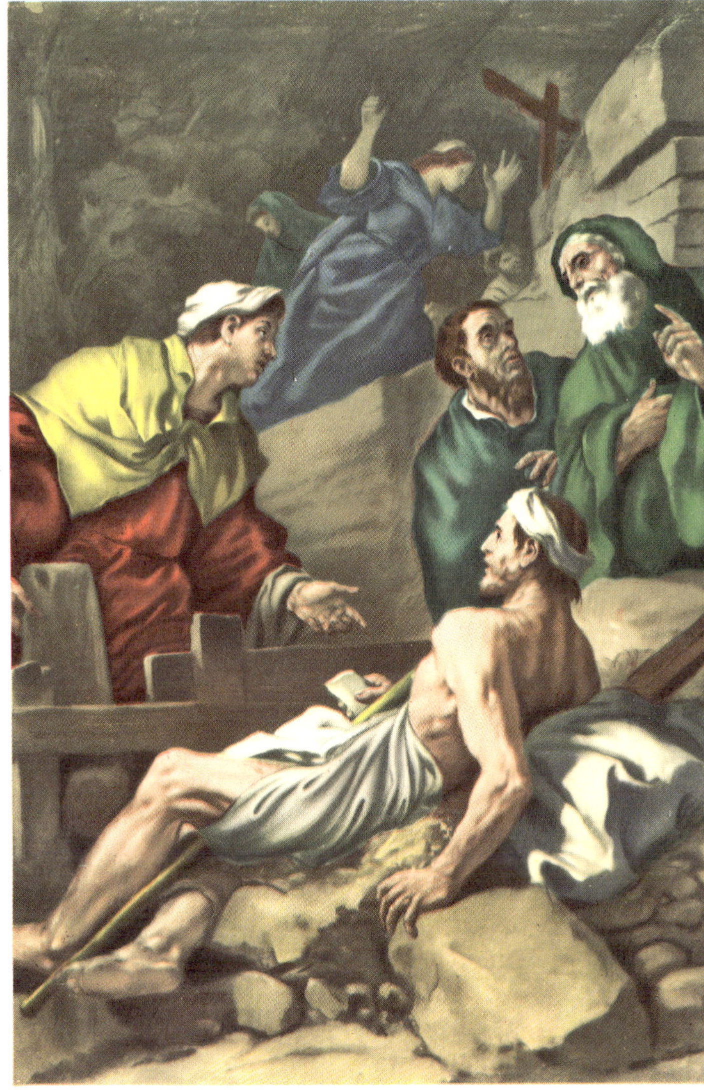

*Job* Giordano-Anderson

In the story of Job, the Holy Bible gives us an outstanding example of patience.

Job was a good, upright man whom God had blessed with everything desirable on this earth: great honor, immense wealth, and a large family.

To test his virtue, however, the Lord permitted one misfortune after another to befall him. First, his property was stolen from him, then all his children perished tragically, and finally he himself was afflicted with an ulcer so terrible that his presence was unbearable to others.

When three of his friends came to him and found him sitting on a dunghill, scraping his sores, they added to his afflictions by accusing him of having merited them by his sins.

Job bore everything in holy patience. He did not complain with the Lord when he lost all that was dear to him, nor even when he was unjustly accused by those who should have comforted him.

And God rewarded him by restoring him to health, blessing him with a new family, and giving him double his former wealth.

Charity demands that we have patience with those who treat us unjustly, with those who are annoying, quarrelsome, fretful or domineering, and with those who are ungrateful and unkind. We all have faults and must bear each other's defects of character patiently, for the love of God. "Learn of me," said Christ, "for I am meek and humble of heart" (Mt. 11:29).

**"The virtue of patience is the one which most assures us of perfection."**

St. Francis de Sales

*Joseph Pardons His Brothers* Schnorr

***What is the sixth spiritual work of mercy?***

**The sixth spiritual work of mercy is to forgive all injuries.**

After having been sold into slavery by his jealous brothers, Joseph, the beloved son of the Patriarch Jacob, rose to be viceroy of Egypt, a position in which he could have easily revenged himself had he so wished. When his brothers came to Egypt seeking food because of a famine that had struck the country, they presented themselves before him without even recognizing him. But Joseph recognized them and, being unable to conceal his emotion, sent everyone from the room so that no stranger would be present when he revealed his identity. Then with deep affection, he said to them, "I am Joseph, your brother. Come closer to me. Do not be distressed nor angry with yourselves that you sold me here, for God sent me before you to deliver you in a striking way." And Joseph kissed and embraced all his brothers, weeping over each one of them. This is the vengeance of the saints: forgiveness!

Sincere forgiveness of those who have offended us is explicitly commanded by Jesus: "For if you forgive men their offenses, your heavenly Father will also forgive you your offenses" (Mt. 6:14-15).

We must always show ourselves ready and quick to forgive wholeheartedly, thus making it easier for him who has offended us to perform his duty of apologizing and making reparation. We cannot seek revenge, for our Lord has said: "Vengeance is mine, I will repay" (Rom. 12:19).

**"If your brother sin, rebuke him; and if he repent, forgive him. And if seven times in the day, he sin against you, and seven times in the day turn back to you, saying, 'I repent'; forgive him."** Lk. 17:34

***What is the seventh spiritual work of mercy?***

**The seventh spiritual work of mercy is to pray for the living and the dead.**

While giving burial to some of his men fallen in battle, Judas Maccabeus, courageous leader of the Israelites, discovered under their coats idolatrous objects forbidden to the Jews by the law. At sight of them, he and his followers betook themselves to prayer, begging God to forgive the slain men's sin. Then the valiant leader took up a collection and sent twelve thousand drachmas of silver to Jerusalem for sacrifice to be offered for the sins of the dead.

The account of this incident in the holy Bible closes with the words: "It is therefore a holy and wholesome thought to pray for the dead, that they may be loosed from sins" (2 Mc. 12:46).

*Judas Maccabeus* Conti

Prayer is the precious key which unlocks the treasures of divine mercy.

St. Paul exhorts us to pray for everyone: "I urge that supplications, prayers, intercessions and thanksgivings be made for all men; for kings, and for all in high positions, that we may lead a quiet and peaceful life in all piety and worthy behavior. This is good and agreeable in the sight of God our Savior, who wishes all men to be saved and come to the knowledge of the truth" (1 Tm. 2:1-5).

In this passage St. Paul states that prayer is a useful and efficacious means for the evangelization of mankind and for their eternal salvation. Through prayer we can invoke the mercy of God upon sinners, and obtain for everyone light, an increase of faith, fervor and perseverance in good.

**"Pray for one another, that you may be saved. For the unceasing prayer of a just man is of great avail."** Jas. 5:16

# INDEX

## Daughters of St. Paul

**IN MASSACHUSETTS**
50 St. Paul's Ave., Jamaica Plain, Boston, MA 02130; **617-522-8911.**
172 Tremont Street, Boston, MA 02111; **617-426-5464; 617-426-4230.**
**IN NEW YORK**
78 Fort Place, Staten Island, NY 10301; **212-447-5071; 212-447-5086.**
59 East 43rd Street, New York, NY 10017; **212-986-7580.**
625 East 187th Street, Bronx, NY 10458; **212-584-0440.**
525 Main Street, Buffalo, NY 14203; **716-847-6044.**
**IN NEW JERSEY**
Hudson Mall — Route 440 and Communipaw Ave.,
Jersey City, NJ 07304; **201-433-7740.**
**IN CONNECTICUT**
202 Fairfield Ave., Bridgeport, CT 06604; **203-335-9913.**
**IN OHIO**
2105 Ontario Street (at Prospect Ave.), Cleveland, OH 44115; **216-621-9427.**
25 E. Eighth Street, Cincinnati, OH 45202; **513-721-4838; 513-421-5733.**
**IN PENNSYLVANIA**
1719 Chestnut Street, Philadelphia, PA 19103; **215-568-2638.**
**IN VIRGINIA**
1025 King Street, Alexandria, VA 22314; **703-683-1741; 703-549-3806.**
**IN FLORIDA**
2700 Biscayne Blvd., Miami, FL 33137; **305-573-1618.**
**IN LOUISIANA**
4403 Veterans Memorial Blvd., Metairie, LA 70002; **504-887-7631; 504-887-0113.**
1800 South Acadian Thruway, P.O. Box 2028, Baton Rouge, LA 70821; **504-343-4057; 504-381-9485.**
**IN MISSOURI**
1001 Pine Street (at North 10th), St. Louis, MO 63101; **314-621-0346; 314-231-1034.**
**IN ILLINOIS**
172 North Michigan Ave., Chicago, IL 60601; **312-346-4228; 312-346-3240.**
**IN TEXAS**
114 Main Plaza, San Antonio, TX 78205; **512-224-8101; 512-224-0938**
**IN CALIFORNIA**
1570 Fifth Ave., San Diego, CA 92101; **619-232-1442.**
46 Geary Street, San Francisco, CA 94108; **415-781-5180.**
**IN HAWAII**
1143 Bishop Street, Honolulu, HI 96813; **808-521-2731.**
**IN ALASKA**
750 West 5th Ave., Anchorage, AK 99501; **907-272-8183.**

**IN CANADA**
3022 Dufferin Street, Toronto 395, Ontario, Canada.

**IN ENGLAND**
128, Notting Hill Gate, London W11 3QG, England.
133 Corporation Street, Birmingham B4 6PH, England.
5A-7 Royal Exchange Square, Glasgow G1 3AH, England.
82 Bold Street, Liverpool L1 4HR, England.

**IN AUSTRALIA**
58 Abbotsford Rd., Homebush, N.S.W. 2140, Australia